# WHEN BIG TREES FALL

## HUTCH PRESTON

ISBN: 0692133216
ISBN-13: 978-0692133217

To all of those who are hurting, tired, and worn, I pray my story helps you find the peace you seek, through a Savior who is ready to lift you up with His righteous right hand.

"Do not fear, for I am with you; Do not anxiously look about you, for I am your God. I will strengthen you, surely I will help you, Surely I will uphold you with My righteous right hand." Isaiah 41:10

# CONTENTS

# ACKNOWLEDGMENTS

First and foremost, thank you to my Lord for allowing me to stay here and share my story. There are so many people that make this possible. I'm here because of the dedication and love of you all. To my Wife and Sons, My Father, Mother, Brothers and Extended Family, Friends, Hunting Buddies, First Responders, Life Flight Pilots, Nurses, Doctors, Surgeons, Physical Therapists, CNAs, and a multitude of Prayer Warriors…I say a heartfelt thank you. If God uses this book to touch and change just one person, it was all worth it, you played a huge part, and I'd do it all over again.

# FOREWORD

# BY MEGHAN PRESTON

In August of 2000, I left my hometown of Fort Smith, AR, and headed up "the Hill" to begin college at the University of Arkansas at Fayetteville. Hutch had recalled meeting me the previous spring, but all I remember from that encounter was some random guy (Hutch) asking me to get his rubber band ball down from some random high place he had thrown it. As a very vertically challenged, senior in high school girl, I just laughed and gave him a funny look. Little did he know he would still be getting that funny look 18 years later. As it would turn out, we ended up seeing each other after I moved to the U of A, and had ample time to talk and get to know each other. Of course, when in college with people from literally everywhere, one of your first "get to know you" conversations is usually about your hometown. I'm pretty sure ours went like this,

"I'm Meghan and I'm from Fort Smith. I love shopping at the mall and drinking milky way mochas at the coffee shop with friends."

"I'm Hutch and I'm from Smackover. I love hunting and being outdoors with my family. My biggest deer is mounted in my living room! It's just 3 months away from modern gun season!"

I'm 100% sure I had not heard of Smackover, Arkansas and I knew nothing about hunting, deer meat, or the outdoors. And while he had heard of Fort Smith, he was not a frequent visitor to any mall or coffee shops.

We were, and still are, as different as night and day. As time would go on, and our relationship would evolve, I realized he really did love hunting...almost as much as he loved me! To be honest, it was (and still is at times) a little bit of a culture shock for me. I grew up in a family that didn't hunt. And I honestly couldn't even tell you of a single location to hunt in my hometown or in Northwest Arkansas where we have been since college. But, he loves it, and I respect that. I love shopping and good coffee shops, and he respects that.

The next decade or so of our lives were typical. Hutch and I did the usual life plan...graduation, marriage, a house, a baby, etc. It wasn't without life being its normal rollercoaster, but for the most part it was good. I held onto a couple of my own life mottos during those years, "if you work hard enough, you can make things happen" and "I can do things by myself" (a spin-off of my very first sentence as a young tot of "I can do it me byself.") I can see now where God had his hand in our lives, to plan and prepare for the "big tree to fall" years later. While in college, we made some very close friends. I had prayed my first year in college that God would send me some good friends. I had great friends all throughout my childhood, but they weren't at college with me. I needed friends that I could walk through everyday life with. Lo and behold, God answered that prayer. He sent us the absolute best group of friends I could ever ask for. These are the friends that in the midst of the trials during Hutch's accident, would be our biggest prayer warriors. I would text them at the most random times with the most random prayer requests, and I knew that they would stop and lift us up in prayer. They would show up to the hospital and rehab during some of our lowest points, when we needed them the most. They made us laugh, they made us cry happy tears, and they made a very difficult time so much easier. They took care of our house, walked and fed our dog, traveled across the country, across the state, slept in hospital and rehab rooms, and kept interstate 40 warm. I always knew we were loved, and incredibly blessed, but when you see your family and friends taking on your burdens and lightening your load in every way possible…it just leaves you speechless. If you don't have people in your life to help pick you up when your life has fallen apart, I encourage you to pray that God will send you that type of person into your life.

All through the times prior to Hutch's accident, I stuck to the mottos I mentioned previously. For the most part, it worked for me. I worked hard to follow our life plan, and did most things without depending on others. As most people experience at some point in their lifetime, God has a way of throwing curve balls that completely take you out of your comfort zone.

The day of Hutch's accident was a normal day for me. I did not have any bad feelings that anything was about to happen. I had packed my car for a weekend away in Fort Smith, took Dax to his sitter, and headed off to teach twenty Kindergartners. You know…you just never know when you are going to get one of those phone calls that completely changes your world. It is probably one of the most vividly remembered events of my life. I was sitting at a table working on math skills with a small group of students, when my brother-in-law called me. He said Hutch had fallen and broken his leg. My first thought was, "well that stinks, but I'm sure he will head to the hospital, get a cast or boot, and head back to his dad's house." The second phone call was not what I had expected, and was about to turn our little lives upside down. My brother-in-law had called again, and said they were flying Hutch to UAMS in Little Rock with broken legs and arms.

After a short cry session in the bathroom, and a talk with my principal, I left work. I picked up Dax from the sitter, headed to meet up with my mom and grandma, and then started down the road to Little Rock. I remember calling my Aunt Sherry and my cousin Brandon on the way, and both of them had the sweet, selfless response, "Well you can stay with us as long as you need to." Little did both of them know, they would have a three-year-old, 7-month pregnant person, and eventually a newborn invading their homes. When people say they don't know how I made it through this experience…I give a big part of the credit to my Aunt Sherry, Uncle Ken, cousins Brandon and Julie, and Hutch's brother and sister-in-law, Wayne and Kristi. They all pitched in and provided normalcy, love, prayers, a roof over our heads, home cooked meals, and many other things for Dax, Dyar, and me throughout our four month stay in Central Arkansas. It honestly made a difficult time almost seem easy for a momma who normally lives away from family. By the time I made it to Little Rock, Hutch was already in his first of ten surgeries. You read that right…TEN surgeries!

For the next four months, our new normal was taking a three year old (and eventually a newborn) to visit his daddy in the hospital and rehab facility, and trying to help him comprehend what would have to become a temporary normal for him. We celebrated multiple holidays in those places. We decorated a Christmas Tree, a gingerbread train, and Santa came there. I don't think I'll ever decorate a gingerbread without remembering the year we were decorating a gingerbread train in Hutch's rehab center. Dax, our three year old was a trooper. We were trying so hard to have a normal Christmas, but Christmas away from home is just tough. But this boy...he smiled and was thankful and joyful throughout the entire situation. He never complained, never whined. He rolled with the punches whatever they were. He continues to roll with the punches. His peppermint stick broke one time and he said, "Mom, it's okay. It works even better now that it's broken." I want to be more like him. He can bring sunshine to any day. He was a true blessing in the midst of this trial.

It was during this time that I realized my life mottos I mentioned above were not really going to work anymore...no matter how hard I tried to stick to them. I've always believed in God and prayer, but I also believed that I could make things happen on my own, and was guilty of taking control of life without trusting Him. After Hutch was released from the hospital, I learned for probably the first time in my life that I have zero control, and that I have to fully rely on God to fill all of our needs. I was over eight months pregnant at that time, and because of the pregnancy, we were told our family would need extra assistance for the next few months since I would also be recovering. So, Hutch's brother Wayne and his wife Kristi invited us to move in with them so that they could help with Hutch, Dax, the new baby, and me! Bless them! This also allowed us to stay in close proximity with UAMS, and Hutch's amazing medical team. Shortly after moving in with them Hutch had an appointment at UAMS with two of his doctors. At this time he could not get in a car…in fact, he was unable to even sit up on the side of the bed. Therefore the only option to get him to this appointment would be in an ambulance. I figured that since we had to pay for an ambulance transport to the appointments, that I would call and at least try to get the appointments back to back. You know…kill two birds with one stone. Well, trying to work with scheduling at UAMS is unfortunately not as fantastic as their hospital and doctors! They claimed the appointments could not be backed up to each other. That was my first experience with hitting a dead end no matter how hard I tried to prevent that happening. So, at this point I was looking at having to get two separate ambulances on two separate days. To do list item #2: Schedule the ambulance for these two appointments. I've always been a fan of having a plan, and a schedule. I could handle whatever was thrown at me as long as I could have a plan, a schedule, and a to-do list. I call the ambulance company, and they told me that they could possibly pick Hutch up for the appointment, but that there was no guarantee. Evidently they only had one ambulance for their region, and if they got a call they would have to cancel Hutch's ride to UAMS that day. Now, I had hit two potential dead ends. Never in my life had I been told a no and a maybe that held so much weight, and so much importance. I took a step back, had a pity-party cry session, and then had to pull myself back together. I realized I had to put my faith in God completely. No more "I do it me byself" or "I'll work hard, be persistent, and they will eventually give in to my need". I had no other option. I had been completely stripped of any power or control of most aspects of our lives. It was such a difficult realization for me, but one I'll never forget. Come to find out, the ambulance was able to pick up Hutch, and by the time he had the next appointment he was in a rehabilitation center. The rehab center provided transportation, and scheduling for all appointments. I was so thankful and relieved to have their help with that part of this process! As much as I wanted to be able to care for Hutch and everyone and everything, and as much as it hurt to admit that I couldn't do it all and needed help...that rehab center was a huge turning point for Hutch's recovery. I do not even want to think about how different life would have turned out without Southern Trace Rehab.

Fast forward two months from Hutch's accident, and we welcomed another bouncing, baby boy into our lives, into a very different life and environment than what our first son had been born into. When Dyar was born, we were living a very unideal life. Hutch was in rehab learning how to walk and facing more surgeries, and the boys and I were living with family three hours from home. We were stressed, worried, and heartbroken that Dyar was entering our life when our life had taken an unexpected turn. When I look at how things have turned out I can't help but be thankful...

thankful for prayers,

thankful for prayer warrior friends from all stages of life,

thankful for an amazing family...the ones who let us live with them...the ones who babysat our children...the ones who sat with us for hours upon hours in hospital rooms and surgery waiting rooms...and the ones who were always there to pick up the pieces when everything would fall apart.

Our children, and Hutch and I are happy and healthy. I only feel we are happy and healthy because of the love, support, and prayers of friends, family, and even complete strangers who have prayed us through the most challenging experience of our lives. God had never left our sides through all of the surgeries, string of bad news, hospital visits, rehab visits, and living with family three hours from home. That was evident in our lives throughout this entire experience. Some days were very difficult, some were easier, but they all brought unexpected blessings. We certainly had a lot of discouraging moments when he was having surgery every few days...but those were the times we saw God show through in the mightiest ways. We have learned that people are so very good, nurses and doctors fulfilling their mission in life are a blessing, and that family will do for you far more than you expect or deserve. We continue to learn daily from this life changing and altering accident. It has definitely been a crazier journey than we could have ever imagined.

The other huge realization I had from this experience came from passing people on the interstate and thinking, "I wish I could be them. They are going to work, meeting people for lunch, and going about their normal days." I then reflected on my life. How many times had I complained about "having" to get up and go to work, about getting up extra early to drop off a child at the sitter on my way to work, about long meetings, and long days, and other things that are just part of a regular normal, daily life? Now, one day, one situation, opened my eyes to the importance of finding joy, and things to be thankful for in the normal, mundane, everyday life. There were many moments I could hardly see a minute ahead, and I did not have any words in my head or heart for prayers. If you are going through rough times I promise it will get better, and when you reflect on the past you will be able to see you were never alone.

I encourage you all to be thankful... thankful for the normal...thankful for crazy mornings trying to rush children out the door for school...thankful for stressful days at work...thankful to be spending evenings at home with your family...thankful for crazy schedules.  Day after day of work, taking care of kids, church...all things we are thankful to have, but tend to take for granted. The daily grind can get exhausting! Sometimes all we need is just a little reminder of how far we have come, and how great it is to be living in the normalcy that anyone can be forced out of for a season. For that means your family is healthy...and that you are blessed more than you could ever imagine...and that you are getting to live the best "normal" you know! Sitting in a surgery room in surgery after surgery and hearing bad news after more bad news will make you yearn for the craziness of your normal life. We have much to be thankful for...even in the midst of exhaustion, storms, and worry! Someone with infertility would love to have children driving them crazy, someone sitting at a hospital would love to have the stress of work, and someone working would love to be at home with their children, someone single would love to have a spouse to be frustrated with. So friends...just be thankful! Count your blessings!

"For I know the plans I have for you declares The Lord. plans to prosper you and not to harm you, plans to give you hope and a future." Jeremiah 29:11

# 1

# IN THE WOODS: THE BEGINNING

To a boy in the South there is nothing like spending a day in the woods. That's right, "woods." Not forest, timberland, or whatever other proper term for a collection of trees. It's bushes, thorns, wild animals, and in our case, mosquitoes that were the size of those old annoying crows that flew over your deer stand just in time to scare something off. For me, the woods are a place I run to. A place I can go ride with the windows down and smell the seasons as they turn in the trees; catching a sniff of air and aromas of South Arkansas crude oil in the breeze. They are a place where I ride shotgun with my dad or brothers...a sanctuary of Peace and Comfort. We go there to hunt, relax, knock off some steam, and shoot old cans with our .22 rifle in the old Smackover Creek. We are horrible shots but I remember once as a child riding out to shoot with Bro. Bill Black, one of my dad's great friends, who had mounted a scope to his rifle which made hitting those cans much easier. The woods were also filled with life lessons. As I grew out of spankings and into my high school years, I knew if my dad showed up to school in the truck, with a brown paper bag full of a six pack of Coke, and just as many oatmeal pies…it was going to be a long ride. Somehow my dad had those ways of making me understand. He would eat, yell a little, eat a little more, calm down some, and depending on what I did and how bad it was, hopefully there was a Coke or two and an oatmeal pie left for me. The fact is anyone who is anyone in Union County Arkansas knows what I'm talking about. The woods are a sacred place to most. Whether it's shooting your first buck, learning to drive on the old roads, or just spending time with your family and friends, you can't explain the feeling until you have lived it.

I remember the day I shot my first deer. Truth be told, I'm not completely sure I was the brightest kid around. I wouldn't say I was short any french-fries or anything, but I can definitely say I've gained a few levels of intelligence over the years. The day was November 19, 1994. We got up that morning and put as many layers on as we could, and headed out just past the Smackover city limits sign to our deer lease. I was prepared to sit with my dad, as I normally did, for the morning hunt. I never had the chance to shoot at many deer. The reason for me never shooting wasn't because of a cold finger, but mainly that I was equipped with a twenty gauge shotgun. Now, looking back on things, I could have sworn to anyone that I had a bazooka. I had no clue that the effective range for a round of buckshot in that gun was no greater than about twenty-five yards...and was being handled by someone with the equivalent to my self-proclaimed "expert" shooting abilities. I mean, in the best conditions and on my best day, little did I know I could barely be accurate at only about a tenth of the distance that we could actually see down the shooting lane.

That being said, with as much talking and moving as I did, a deer would practically have to be deaf before it would come within a hundred yards of us. Nonetheless, I wouldn't have traded anything for those moments. On that particular day though, my hawk-like vision spotted movement about two-hundred yards away. Excited, more than ever, I slapped my dad's leg and said "DEER!" and pointed down through the trees. The moment I got "Deh" out of my mouth my dad already had his gun up across me with his scope down the line. I remember being a little disappointed that he wouldn't let me shoot, but then again, I didn't realize I couldn't actually shoot that far. You know, the older I get, I'm starting to realize that may have been part of his plan. I refuse to accept that it was because my dad was being mean. I relate it to the reality of how much we relied on venison to live each year. I'm sure he didn't want me scaring away anything with my pebble and sling shot. I have peace knowing that if a deaf, three legged, blind deer walked out to our left side at about ten yards or less, I would have gotten the shot…I hope. Anyway, as my dad looked through the scope I was on the edge of my seat. Squeezing my fingers in my ear and waiting for the bang. Then I felt his belly shake. He was laughing. The "deer" I saw were about six turkeys moving through. Therein lies the true reason for me carrying my glorified slingshot. I hung my head low and he comforted me as any father would. Then as any other dad would he poked fun at me again. Finally about an hour later I did see movement again and it was a deer for sure. Actually I saw it because I was whipped in the eye by my dad's elbow as he flung his gun up to get ready for a potential shot. I guess I was so down about the turkey incident that I wasn't really paying attention anymore. When I saw the deer, well any deer, I would get really excited. I wanted my dad to be successful. I wanted him to have the biggest deer in the woods so I could brag and tell my friends about it. For some reason, as the deer is making its way across the lane my dad asked ME if I could see any antlers. For a more unknown reason, I said emphatically "Yes it's an eight point! At least an eight point!" A shot soon followed and the deer ran away. Upon tracking the deer we started seeing tracks that indicated the deer may have been a doe. Back then you had to have a special doe permit to even harvest one and thank the Lord we did. My dad kept asking "are you sure it was a buck?" "Yes Dad!" Then he'd laugh and say "well do you remember the turkeys?" I didn't find it as funny as he did. After a few more yards of tracking we walked up on the old doe. No antlers. All I could see was my dad and a sheepish grin on his face. I think he wanted to joke with me again but he knew I had reached my fun threshold for the morning. We loaded up the deer and did what we had to do.

Later that day it became time to go out for the afternoon hunt. Dad let me know how exhausted he was from carrying out and dressing the "eight point doe" he shot earlier that morning. I was itching to get back out, and he didn't care to. In an effort to please me he decided he'd let me hunt by myself on an old deer stand that sits behind our house. It sits half in the woods. By half I mean literally half. You can see the stand from our kitchen window where my dad and mom were cooking deer chili. I was eagerly determined to prove to my dad that just because there hasn't been an actual deer harvested or even seen from that spot in over fifteen years, I was going to somehow find a way to attract one with my hunting expertise. On my way out of the house for my lengthy walk of about thirty yards; I realized that my firearm was barely going to shoot a squirrel out of a tree. Although happy about the opportunity to hunt by myself, I quickly realized how much of a disadvantage I had and maybe I was being set up. Pacified, you know? I could hear my brother Cliff and friend Bryan playing basketball next to our house. Not only did I not have sufficient fire power, but I was now being forced to overcome the constant pounding of a basketball, and loud trash talking that could potentially scare away any deer that even so much as thought about coming close enough for me to shoot. I expressed my concerns with my dad and he decided to hand me the family .308. A rifle! I didn't know what to do with it. I immediately felt like Ralphie with his BB gun. Although I was just barely fourteen, and most teens my age were well versed in the use of these things, this was a very big deal to me. So much that I completely forgot about the promise that I'd never see any deer. I'm thinking that was my dad's plan as well. I really don't think he ever expected me to shoot the gun anyway.

Now, I need you to understand that in our neck of the woods we shoot to eat. It's true that we all search for big bucks, but the point of hunting is for food. By chance, if a big buck lives long enough to grow into a monster buck, and happens to re-define the horrible gene pool we have, then of course we will fire away and be happy. Sadly, the odds of us shooting a high scoring monster buck are very slim. Spoiler alert…when I tell the story of my monster buck, in our eyes, it's a monster buck. To this day I have yet to harvest one that's even close to this one. "Once in a lifetime bucks," are usually what they are referred to. I'm here to tell you they live up to their name.

I sat down about 3:45 p.m. and was feeling very anxious

and surprisingly tired. I tried to fight through the dozing off as much as I could. I mean, now that I had access to this high powered rifle; I had this newly born confidence that a monster buck would magically walk out and save the day. I needed to fight hard to stay awake and be alert. So much was riding on this hunt for me. I remember taking time to pray that God would send me a buck. Being that we used the only doe tag we had on this morning's eight point I had no other choice. I wanted everyone to be proud of me; so I specifically remember praying for an eight point with three main tines on each side of his frame. As crazy as it seemed, I truly believed I would kill a big buck that afternoon. Y'all, I honestly don't remember when I fell asleep. I guess it was God's natural way of keeping me quiet and still. At around 4:30, I woke up to a buck standing about seventy-five yards from me, and walking across my shooting lane. It was the only open shooting lane we had back there; and if, and when he got across there's no way I'd have another shot at him. So, in normal Hutch fashion I got really excited, did a big Barney Fife panic, actually stood up and raised the gun. For those of you who have never actually hunted those are three big "no no's." I can only imagine God sent the perfect blind and deaf buck in North America out to Smackover that day. I could clearly see with my naked eye that he had eight points with his three tines on each side. He had already crossed the shooting lane and was staring at me through a group of trees. I'm still standing in the deer stand-completely exposed to nature- and most likely wetting myself at this point. That's "no no" number four by the way. By now, regardless of three mistakes and one debatable that I'll never fully admit to, I was determined to stay still and see what his next movement was. I remember praying again, "God this is the deer for me, and I've ruined this already but please let him come back across." It was at that moment, for reasons unknown, this beautiful buck whose vision, eye sight, smell, and mental state have yet to be determined, made a turn and slowly walked back across my shooting lane. I remember my older brother Dave explaining to me the exact steps in shooting a deer through a scope with precision and those very words of wisdom rang through my head "just as soon as you see the deer in the scope, pull the trigger." Ha! That's exactly what I did. The deer ran about twenty or so yards, and it was a moment I will never forget. When we walked up to him my dad's reaction was great. See, he just watched the whole event through the kitchen window and was actually glad I didn't shoot myself or anyone else. We also noticed that the buck was actually a ten point with four tines on each side. The deer was bigger than I had asked for.

In the years after this event I have realized the magnitude of what happened that day. It reminds me of the verses in the book of Matthew that talk about a childlike faith. I know many people have a difference of opinions about what that scripture actually refers to, however, when we really think about it, we can all learn a valuable lesson. I watch my oldest son Dax, and as he gets older I've realized you can tell him anything and he actually believes it. He has no life experience to question or judge his experiences or my advice from. All he is left with is my word and he has to take it for what he assumes it is worth. At his age, his father's advice and information is worth its weight in gold. He has faith that what I say is true, and lives his young life based on the information he soaks in. This same faith points back to this day when I harvested this deer. I truly believed I was going to see a huge buck that afternoon. I prayed and specifically asked for this animal to appear, and believed it would happen. Despite everything I did wrong at the time God still honored my faith and found fitting, at this moment, to provide me with what I asked for. Does this mean God will always give you what you think you need? I think we all know the answer to that. What I can tell you is this event changed the way I thought about life and prayer. This single situation set me up for a list of events, over the next nineteen or so years, that would truly change my world and how I perceived it.

2

# THE OLD PEACH TREE

I know it sounds cliché but growing up, for the most part, was relatively easy. As a family in our early years I'm sure we went through some struggles but, in my opinion, our parents did a good job of hiding it from us. Maybe they didn't hide it as much; they just tried their best to live a happy life and to teach us to be content with what we had. We didn't have as much as the other kids had. Our dad, a minister, pastored various churches. We even had a few years traveling with him while he was preaching evangelism services. Money was scarce at that time. As I've become older, I have come to the realization that churches don't value their pastors enough. There were times when my dad would come home and be a wreck. Emotionally exhausted from being the listening ear of complaints, sorrows, and any other burden from his church he was forced to bear. "That comes with the territory!" people say. I know that, but a pastor's work is a twenty-four hour, seven day a week job where he is expected to be on call at all times. Always ready to answer and solve problems, make hospital visits during his own family time, talk someone through marital problems and show up late for his own family events because of it. All of this for the glory of God, yes, but for pennies. Not that money matters… but at the very least a pastor should be able to make enough money to make his ends meet…and I'm not talking about mismanaging money, Y'all, I mean "bologna sandwich for dinner, paint your own swoosh on your dollar store shoes" pennies. Even still, at the first sign that a pastor is failing or letting his guard down, he's got a group of deacons or angry church members beating on his office door ready to form a search committee to find a new one. Meanwhile, he's struggling to pay his bills, feed his children, and save his marriage…while you're upset because he was late to your child's wisdom tooth pulling procedure. Am I angry? No, but hopefully you see where I'm going with this. We, as a church, put a mountain of pressure on our pastors and church staff. At the first sign of failure we throw them to the curb, make room for the next guy and force our unrealistic expectations on him, only to have him fall into the same trap. After about four or five different pastors we turn and blame society and the world for our problems rather than turning our finger around and pointing it at ourselves. We have all fallen into this misconception that pastors are superhuman and never get tempted or tried in life. If their personal life actually gets exposed, they are labeled as a false prophet or "well he just wasn't who we thought he was." You know why? It's because we use our spiritual leaders as a crutch, Y'all. We struggle so much in our own lives, that we have to have a person to look up to and measure ourselves against, or have a physical example of a strong person to lean on. We call THAT Faith. We rely on a person to go to when all else fails. An earthly person to heal us…to bring us out of our depths. Are pastors good to help? Sure. But as soon as we start relying on them in the place of

God, when they do fail us, because they're actually human and NOT God, and our standards for them are above the realm of what they can physically accomplish, we throw a fit because we no longer have the crutch we thought we had. We get angry because they've failed us and messed up the mojo in our own life. We forget that we have a Savior that takes care of that for us. Why? Because we've put our Faith in man. That's not Faith. Our spiritual leaders are not our ultimate healers. They are called to lead, yes, to be shepherds, yes, but they are not miracle workers. If we keep pounding our leaders into the ground because of unrealistic expectations, then who will lead us? I ask for you to take a look into your own life. Stop now and say a prayer for your spiritual leaders, ask the Lord how you can pray for them, and ask that He show you how to experience and exercise true Faith. Also, what problems and sins do you struggle with? What would you do if you found out your pastor or spiritual leader struggled with the same issues? Would you be the first to point a finger? Pray silently? Attempt to help? I'm only ranting because I've seen it firsthand. No one really knows the life of a minister until you have lived with or as one. My family, for a time, had it lucky. We were surrounded with good people and able to make ends meet. It wasn't typical, and we never expected it to be. As I mentioned before, we were taught to be content with our situation. God would provide what we needed and He did. We had many trials, but they all served as learning experiences.

I remember being out on the evangelism trail with my dad as he was preaching in a church in Northeast Louisiana. I couldn't tell you the name of it now, but I believe Cliff and I were about eight and nine years old at the time. That would have put Dave around fourteen. We weren't perfect, but we were expected to be gentlemen. Sometimes things got the best of us. On this particular night of the revival there was a packed house. As always, we sat with our mom on the first to second row of the church, and listened attentively. This night was a little different. About half way through the service a poor gentleman in the row behind us had something lodged in his nose. To this day we still don't exactly know what was in there. By the sound of it we would guess a rhino, but that is still up for debate. Regardless, the man spent a good eight minutes trying to get it out of his nose. I still feel the breeze of the snorts and shews that ensued. Those eight minutes, to us three boys, felt as long as the everlasting eternity in which our dad was preaching about during the service. On about snort four of the rhino extraction attempt, Cliff lost it with a snort of his own. Once this happened we all three lost it. Our heads were bobbing up from the pews like an advanced level game of whack-a-mole. Our mom, trying to keep a straight face, started slapping our heads to get us to stop. I believe the scene was described as our heads appearing to be church bells ringing as our mom gently popped them from behind. We can all notice our dad preaching away at the pulpit, and he started cutting eyes. That didn't help. About the time we would finally get calmed down; the poor rhino would try to climb back up the man's nose, and he'd snort it out again. By this point, our mom was in on it too. She was laughing just as hard as we were. Her hand was over her mouth. Dave's face is beet red. Cliff has now made it into the floor, and I'm in the middle crying rhino sized tears of laughter. Just then, a thunderous voice came from above. It wasn't God...but our dad. In the midst of this great sermon, he had noticed all four of us had now apparently opened our own circus in row two of this church. He politely calls our mom up to the front of the church and whispers for a good two minutes. In the meantime, the guy with the animal in his nose is still fighting, we are still laughing, Cliff is trying to hand the guy a tissue underneath the pew, and it's just getting bad all around. The best part was our mom coming back to relay the message from our dad and trying to keep a straight face. The rest of that night wasn't as fun. It was a long drive back to Arkansas that resulted in dad treating himself to a cheeseburger while we went home and had sandwiches. Well-deserved on both parts. There may or may not have been a potluck that night at the church. I'm not really sure that we would have been invited to stay anyway. We had many, many great moments as a family of five. Again, we didn't have much, but we did our best to live and be happy while doing it.

Our Dad didn't believe in "sparing the rod," as the Bible would say. It can be argued that he took that scripture to heart. Come to think of it, I'm surprised it wasn't hand carved into a five by twenty inch wooden plank that was nailed right under our "As for me and my house, we will serve the Lord" sign that hung above our kitchen sink. All he asked of us was to be respectful, say "Yes Sir, No Sir" and "Yes Ma'am, No Ma'am," love the Lord, and for the most part, we'd be in his good graces. Now don't think we got off easy. "Respect" covered a lot of things. Let's see… there was don't talk back, don't lie, curse, steal, beg, lie, cheat, mess the house up, hit your brother, hit your mother, hit your father, lie, and a host of other things. Did I mention lie? Dad wasn't a fan of lying. You could stick a hair pin in a wall outlet and it would be more pleasant than the repercussions of lying to my Dad. Now he never abused us. Get that out of your mind already. Close? Maybe, Ha! I will attest that it wasn't anything we never deserved. I really believe we turned out to be better men because of it. At least that's what he would say. In all of that, we grew great respect for him. Not fear. Never fear. Instead, a mountain of respect that enables us to have a great relationship today. He's tamed a little, especially with his grandkids. Around two years of age, Dax was having a little trouble listening and it was at a point that he needed some form of adjustment. It wasn't even spanking worthy, but as I approached Dax, Dad calmly, but sternly, mumbled out of the side of his mouth "Don't you spank that baby in my house." I was dumbfounded! "Dad? Are you serious? Do you remember what you did to us in this very house?" "Yes," He'd say, "and you're not doing that to him here!" "Ok Dad, well I wasn't." "Are you talking back to me, Son? You know you're still not too old!" "Wait, what? What is happening? So I can't give spankings, but you can?" "That's exactly right!" he said. I'm still confused. He loves his grand babies.

For Christmas one year Cliff and I got bikes. We traveled everywhere on those things. He was "Ponch" and I was "Jon." We watched a ton of re-runs as kids, Ha! Together we solved many crimes on those blue bikes. Sometimes I think our dad gave us specific rules that he knew would tempt us to break, you know, just to see if we'd listen. A test. Lots of tests around our house. Once I remember it rained like crazy for about two hours. Dave, Cliff and I were up at the school playing a game of football in the massive downpour with a few friends. Dad had given us specific instructions to stay out of the water while riding our bikes. Specifically this puddle that lined the edge of Mt. Holly Rd. This puddle was the mother of all puddles. About forty yards long and I'd estimate at least a foot deep and five yards wide at its widest. I bet it rained an inch in those two hours. After playing football we started riding home. The mother of all puddles had become the father of all puddles. Like mosquitoes flying into a bug zapper, we couldn't stop. It was calling us. I mean, we were already wet, right? I don't remember who went in first. Because he's not here right now, I'll blame it on Cliff. It was utter bliss. The water was half up our legs, Y'all! We could barely pedal. On the right morning we could have probably had an excellent duck hunt out of it. Life was great. About that time, we heard the rumble of a truck coming around the curve. There was nothing we could do. We could see the old blue Chevy with the matching, painted, rarely used boat rack making the curve. We were knee deep both figuratively and literally. It was Dad. By the time he made the curve, we had already dismounted, as if by subconscious reaction and terror we had to do something to explain the situation. I mean, if we're not ON the bikes, were we really riding them in the puddle? We quickly concocted a story of how officers Ponch and Jon had to save drowning puppies…you know, life and death stuff. FYI, that excuse does not hold up in the court of Dr. David H. Preston, Sr. Actually, it probably makes your sentence a little worse. Now I know deep down our dad probably knew riding through that puddle was more fun than we'd had in years. There was most likely a piece of him that wanted to do it too…at least I like to think so. But he never yelled. Never screamed. It was just a simple "Wha'Chall Doin'?" Translation? "What Y'all," or "What are Y'all," or "What are you all doing." You know, for those of you who are curious.

"Rollin' our bikes through the water?"

"Rollin' huh? Y'all take them bikes back to the house and go to your rooms, I'll be home in a little bit."

That was probably the worst response ever. Usually punishment is quick and swift. But this time, he didn't show any anger, just simple instructions. So were we grounded? Unlikely, we never got grounded, Ha! But maybe this one time? Maybe he'd take it easy on us. It was the mystery of what may happen that kept us on the proverbial edge of our seats. By the way, we weren't sitting. For some reason, we actually pushed our bikes all the way home. With our stomachs in knots, we were worried about what our punishment may be…but held out hope that it was only just a long time out. You know, to sit and think about it. Then Cliff mentioned, "I wonder where he's going?" Our friend walking with us said "probably to get a new leather belt." That didn't help. We waited for what seemed like hours. Unbeknownst to us, he was in fact, getting a new leather belt… and we weren't in time out either, Ha! Boy, were we not in time out! On top of that, Ponch and Jon were off duty for at least four weeks. Then again, it did beat the old peach tree limbs that we'd have to choose. One of the happiest days in my life was when dad accidently ran over part of that peach tree and it died, forcing us to have to burn it down. We had a party. By "we" I mean us boys…I believe I saw a tear in dad's eye.

Those weren't the only lessons he taught us in life. When I was seventeen I worked for a local grocery store in El Dorado, Arkansas. It came time for my Dad to get a new truck to help him with traveling. I was informed that I would get his. I couldn't wait for the day he made his purchase so he could hand over the keys to the 1994 F-150 Super Cab with bucket seats. We took many trips through the woods in that truck and shared many life lessons. The day finally came and I stuck out my hand. He laughed at me and said, "It's not going to be that easy! You have a job and when you give me five-hundred dollars, you can have the truck." To say I was disappointed and angry would be an understatement. I didn't understand why he would make me pay for a truck that, thankfully, was paid off and I was clearly entitled to. Reluctantly, over the next few weeks I was able to save up enough to give him what he wanted. With a bit of a seventeen year old attitude I walked into his bedroom and casually threw it on the bed. It's really a wonder that he didn't just throw it right back at me and call the deal off. Instead, he just looked at me and said, "Is that for the truck?"

"Yes, Dad, you know a lot of people's parents don't charge them for their old trucks."

"Son, go get in the truck and let's go ride around."

As I mentioned before, that command usually meant we were heading for a not so fun trip through the woods so he could lay in to me about disrespecting him or doing something I shouldn't have. We pulled out of our driveway and he headed the other direction. I didn't know what was going on. The first stop we made was to a local store and he told the clerks he needed four new tires for the truck and an oil change. When he paid, I noticed he pulled out the five-hundred dollars I had given him and gave a portion of it to the clerk. Talk about feeling like a loser. He could have not said another word or done anything else that day and his point would have been made. Being Dad, he didn't stop there. He still wasn't talking to me, by the way. We just stood there and watched them work on the truck. When we got done there, he drove us to a car wash and paid to have it cleaned. By this point, I was just slumped down in my seat. After the day was over, there was just enough of the five-hundred left to buy us lunch. How did I know this? Because after all of the silence, he broke it by saying, "And you're buying us lunch." When lunch was over he quietly handed me the keys and I almost gave them back. I felt so stupid. He said, "Drive us home!" So I did. On the twenty minute drive back he began to explain to me how fortunate I was to be able to have a good job and buy my first truck. He said, "Son, if I had never made you pay for this truck, you would have never appreciated it. You just saw your hard earned money put new tires on it, get your oil changed, and clean it…now go take care of it."

I'll admit, there have been times in my life that I have mismanaged the advice my father gave and continues to give me. What I can say is that he's always been there to provide us with the necessary tools to get things accomplished in a respectful and godly way. He was tough on us, but those of you who know him also know he's a huge teddy bear. Having children now myself, and looking back on these stories, I know how easy it would have been for Dad to say to himself "You know they're just boys riding their bikes in that big ole' puddle, let them have fun." I'm sure that crossed his mind. But honestly, I thank the Lord that although that most likely crept through Dad's head, he stuck to his guns, knowing he gave us instructions to never ride through that puddle, knowing we knew better, and knowing if he didn't follow through, we'd start losing our respect for authority. Not just his, but anyone's. As Dad would say, "If your children don't learn to respect and obey you, how will they ever learn to respect and obey the Lord?" He just refused to let his boys disrespect him, our Mom, or anyone else. Like instances where he made us pay for old trucks, he felt it was his God given duty to turn us into respected men, and those experiences would help do that. I know my brothers will attest, had it not been for old peach tree limbs and new leather belts, we wouldn't be who we are today. Not saying that's the only way to raise children these days, but seeing the way some people currently act, maybe it needs to be? I know I sure needed it.

3

# WHAT LIFE BRINGS

As years went on, the pressure of life clearly started taking its toll on our family. Some would classify it as letting guards down; and to be honest, I still can't fully comprehend what actually happened. I struggled with sharing this part of my life with you. I don't like to think about it. The sad thing is that I think about it every day. I truly feel that I went through these situations to help other people. It's for that reason that I must share.

On August 16, 1996, I woke up and rolled out of bed. Only a couple of weeks home from my first trip with Lay Witnesses for Christ International. This experience allowed the opportunity to minister to Olympic Athletes in Atlanta, Georgia during the Summer Games. Dave was in Fayetteville at the University of Arkansas. I'm not going to lie…it was hard to be home without him. To this day, my brothers and I have a relationship no one can really explain. The only thing it can be related to is what people describe as the relationships between twin brothers or sisters. There was a link missing and it made life awkward and tough to deal with. On top of that, I struggled with what is now known as panic disorder. I'm not talking about an anxiety attack where your water bill is past due and you temporarily freak out. I'm talking about clinical, emotional, scary, tragic moments that happen for no reason at any given time. I'm in my thirties right now, and I still have issues with them. Cliff also suffers from them, and we have a special bond knowing what each other goes through and how to calm the other down. I've heard it best described as this…"Imagine you are in the woods. It's almost dark, and you're already a little apprehensive. At that moment you see a giant grizzly bear within three feet of you. That feeling you have right then." The most scared feeling you could ever have. This feeling can last for thirty minutes or longer. The sad thing is being as scared as you are of this bear, the bear doesn't even exist. I've gone two weeks without eating because of them. Certain foods can trigger them. Certain events. It's really hard to get out of bed every morning when they are bad. They usually lead to depression, or could even be caused by it. You can have an attack because you are so afraid you will have an attack, that you actually give yourself one. It sounds crazy, but those of you who truly deal with them know what I'm talking about. There are people who think they deal with them, then there are those who truly deal with them. The fear and anxiety are crippling. All of that being said, on this morning, cards were stacked against me to say the least.

When I awoke that morning, I could hear my mom and dad in some form of a misunderstanding. I could tell dad was crying. I worried about everything. So I made my way into the living room to see what I could "help" with. See, Dave had this weird way of calming them both down when they had a disagreement. I just assumed since he wasn't there I could fill that role. I didn't know it would be to the magnitude of what was about to happen. When I walked in I could tell my mom had slept on the couch. My dad was in tears. He said, "Tell him what you're doing." I could tell she didn't want to. At this point I was crying. I knew it wasn't good. She finally said "I've decided to leave." At fifteen and half sheltered, I didn't really know how to take that. My family wasn't supposed to split up like that. I tried my best to talk her into staying and it didn't work. I didn't have Dave there to help. I was the oldest child at home. I remember Cliff was still asleep, so I ran to wake him. I don't really know why I did that other than I knew I didn't want to go through this by myself. In some weird way, if our mom was leaving, I didn't want him to miss it. Not that I had evil plans for him to endure it, but I didn't know if or when she'd be back. My mind was racing…the thought of never seeing my mom again swept through…in my panicked state of mind, I didn't want him to miss out on seeing his mom for the last time. So I got him up, and told him what was going on. He started crying. We all tried to talk her into staying. Finally my dad requested that if she were not going to change her mind, that she go ahead and do what she needed to do. We were all hysterical at this point and needed to be relieved. I remember she went back and packed a small bag. She had just bought a new car and backed it into our driveway. My dad went back to his bedroom and I remember Cliff was laying on our couch crying. Our driveway door made this eerie noise when it opened. You can still hear it open at any point in our house, so it was obvious she was leaving. I remember following her to the door and trying to make her stay. When she shut the door and made her way out, I can remember the devastation that followed. The worst part was hearing my dad scream "NO!" really loud, as if someone were trying to hurt him. I stood there at the door and watched our mom load her bag into the trunk of her car. She blew me a kiss and drove away. This was the last time I would see my mother until a brief visit at Christmas.

As much as I try, I will never forget the details of that morning. It has literally haunted me. I have never felt more devastated, lost, worried, confused, and alone than I did in that moment. If you buy into the lie that your kids will be ok; and in some cases better off if you leave your family, I can assure you they will never forget. Had it not been for my upbringing, and my dad continuously keeping us in the Word, I don't know that I would have made it. I almost didn't. I beat myself up for months. I actually blamed myself. I thought I failed at keeping them together. At fifteen, about to turn sixteen years old, I was ready to end my life because of guilt. If I were able to do my part, they would still be together. That single thought constantly tormented me. The only thing that kept me from ending my life was the simple fact that one of my family members would have to come home and find me. I couldn't imagine doing that to them. As time went on, our dad was able to share his story with a few churches. It was very therapeutic and allowed me to take the blame off of myself. I was able to express my concerns with him, and he explained to me some things that were currently unknown to me. It was by the Grace of God that I pulled through that situation. I'd love to tell you that I was able to let the hurt go, but I can't. My hurt turned into anger, and although I was able to hide it well, I carried it with me for a long time. I can tell you, if this event had never happened, I wouldn't be where I am today. So, as much hurt and heartache as I went through, God still gets the glory. I'll continue to explain.

Life after our mom left had its fair share of down moments. Without our mom's income, it really put a burden on our remaining family to survive. Dave cut his semester short and came home from college for the rest of the year. We both worked at a local grocery store to help make ends meet. I remember every Thursday was our payday. We would both come in and lay our checks on our dad's bed. He never asked for them. It was just something we felt like we needed to do. I really don't know how we would have made it without doing that. A couple of weeks after mom left, two deacons from the church he pastored came to our house to tell my dad "the church" thought it would be best that he resign his position. That came as a very hard blow to us. We felt abandoned. It was hard enough to make life adjustments to our situation, but now, the only people we felt we could rely on had turned their backs on us as well. That's how we felt. Regardless of anyone's opinion or interpretation of scriptures, at that time, we felt abandoned. We all, at this point, knew the reasons why mom had left us and the issues her and our dad had to deal with. For her sake, and for the sake of our parent's relationship if she decided to come home, we did our best to keep it hidden from the public eye as best we could. Because of that, we had to face scrutiny from other churches, believers, etc., who basically turned their backs on us because they didn't have the whole story, so all they were left to do was assume. By assume, I mean assume our family was out of control. "I guess they just weren't who we thought they were." On the other hand, we had a mountain of supporters that fought for us. They were a light of encouragement and help through our darkest time. Those great people are still in our lives today.

We learned to cook, clean, and do our own laundry. We weren't professionals, by any means, but we got the job done. I remember Cliff and me digging our clothes out and putting them in the wash before we went to bed. We would alternate days on who would wake up at six in the morning and put them in the dryer. We'd hop out of the shower and get dressed by our dryer and head out for school each morning. Why we didn't do a whole load at a time, I have no idea. Eventually our Granny Preston would come and take over laundry duties. She did her best to help us along the way. She worked with a sharp attitude and never took no for an answer. Her ultimate goal in life is to take care of us. I remember days she would walk in and scold us because the house didn't look like she wanted it, then come back three days later and cry because it looked perfect and we didn't "need her anymore." We actually got pretty good at knowing what she wanted. To our house, there is a gravel road that is about a tenth of a mile long. We could see her coming. She never drove fast down the driveway, so we knew if we saw her coming we had a good forty-five to fifty seconds before she would get into the house. You'd be surprised what we could accomplish in the short time it took her to get to our house. She did it because she loved us.

As I mentioned before, we did have an overwhelming amount of support. The thing that eats at you most is eventually, your support goes on with their lives. Not that it's a bad thing… it's just a normal human function. Anyone in a tragedy goes through it. When a person or family goes through a situation like this, it's a huge change in their lives. Initially yes, there is a ton of support. Even in the death of a friend or relative, people are always there to support you and comfort you. The hardest part of coping with the tragedy is when those people of comfort naturally go on about their lives. It is the time about four to six weeks after the event…when the initial shock, surprise, and short grieving period is over for those not directly involved. Yet you, the sufferer, are still dealing with your loss or tragedy. In my case, I was still crying every night and everyone else outside of our family had appeared to have moved on. School days were normal. People stopped hugging you wherever you went. It's not that they were insincere, it's just plainly, they had moved on. Somehow we still had to grieve but move on as well. This whole process gave me a feeling of helplessness. I wanted people to feel sorry for me. I wanted people to continue to comfort me. That's what felt good and what was helping. Now I had the feeling of walking blindly through a minefield. Hoping I wouldn't have a meltdown in the middle of school and get reprimanded. That's what I was scared of. I was so afraid seven weeks after my mom left that I'd lose it, emotionally, in the middle of school and some teacher or staff person would tell me to "suck it up and get over it." Would that have happened? Most likely not, but that's what I feared. I was confused as to why God would allow this to happen. If He allowed this to happen, then why would He save me from this fear and anxiety I had every day? Every single day was like a long panic attack. This fear began to control my life. I was stuck adjusting to life without our mom. Our dad was emotionally distraught. Depression was kicking in. He felt like he was a failure, and he was fighting to save whatever he could; as well as, keep some form of a supporting attitude for us. As much as I love my dad, some of my most un-stressful moments were at school because it temporarily took my mind off of things. The weird thing is, I actually feared going to school every day. Tell me how that makes sense? It doesn't. That's just how emotionally wrecked I was.

I remember Christmas time rolled around that year and our mom wanted to see us. We had not seen her since she left, and Dave had not seen her since he left for college that fall. We made our plans to attempt to talk her into coming back. We went to her temporary home nervously praying that somehow we'd be able to convince her into jumping in the car with us and coming home. I remember walking in, and immediately thinking "Wow she's not emotional at all, she has actually moved on." I guess…deep inside…I was wanting her to see us and magically miss home. I really thought there would be some awkward crying and an "I'm sorry" or two but there wasn't. It was honestly as if nothing had ever happened. We went on as planned and brought the issue up. It went so bad that the night ended early. She was upset that we even brought it up, and it made for an uncomfortable night. She was crying when we left, and we cried the whole way home. Surprising as it may be, this event actually helped me move on. I still had a ton of sadness, but this actually made me angry. It gave me the "we can do this" attitude. It didn't make it all better, but it did make it a little easier to function.

It was after this that I realized the importance of trying to find the good out of the situation. The only way my mind and body could actually work was if I came to some sort of epiphany. God showed me ways to divert this tragedy for good. Instead of looking for all of the terrible things that could come out of this, I started focusing on the positives. It didn't release all of the anger and anxiety, but it helped me to cope. It kept my mind occupied. I remember our dad sitting us down and giving us this speech that "No matter what, we are gonna be together and nothing is gonna tear us boys apart. We're gonna fish, hunt, play ball, and do things like normal and move on as best as we can." My dad will be the first to tell you he didn't make perfect decisions during his marriage, but I respect him because he tried. When push came to shove, he tried to make it work.

With this new found confidence, as shaky as it was, we did our best to move on. My focus was trying to find the positives. It's an exercise that I attempt to accomplish to this day. It's hard, it's not fool proof, but when carried out it's very effective. I started writing down reasons why God would allow us to go through this. I reflected on the question, "What good experiences have come as an exact result of this situation?" If this event were to never have happened, these specific things would not have taken place. It's amazingly therapeutic. There were people we would have never met if my mom had not left. Another example, Cliff and his music career would have never happened. There are many things on this list that God would use for His Glory. Although it was not a cure for my sad feelings, anxiety, and anger, it definitely helped me through the tougher times. It was an encouragement that helped me learn to live with what had happened. Although it was never my fault, I was an innocent victim of the tragedy of a few bad decisions. It also helped me to find ways to enjoy the moments we did have with our mom after this experience. God helped us to adjust.

High School continued on. I still had some hidden emotional issues that I was quietly dealing with. The issues clearly took a toll on my grades, but they weren't horrible...well, depending on who you ask, ha! By my Senior Year Dave was back at college at the University of Arkansas. I wanted to follow and my dream was to graduate as a Razorback. I remember going to my guidance counselor at our high school and expressing my wishes. I was quickly shot down. I was given the "you know college isn't for everyone" speech. Seriously, I really was. I remember thinking "Are my grades THAT bad?" Maybe it was a work ethic? I'm really not sure. She suggested that maybe I go to a local community college and I just wasn't having it. She gave me the standard scholarship applications that I assume everyone got to fill out, but that was about it. If I wanted to apply for college, especially THAT college, I was on my own. I guess I don't really blame her, actually, I'm thankful. I don't think she realizes how much she actually pushed me. There's a long line of musical talent in our family. With the help of Dave, I called the Marching Band and scheduled an audition. I realize I was not the best trombonist they've ever had, but by the Grace of God they gave me a scholarship and after a few strings were pulled I was accepted to the University of Arkansas.

My freshman year and through college I had a work study job in the Band Office. My boss was a lady named Connie. I can tell you over the years Connie and I had some knockdown, drag out arguments, but we had even more great times. Contact with my Mom during college was still a little shaky. Dave also worked for Connie, so she knew our situation. To this day I still talk with her, and I don't think she realizes the impact she made on our lives. She was our Mother when we struggled so much with our own. I remember once I had high fever. I wasn't coming in to work. Wasn't going to class. She'd call my dorm room and when I did answer, I could barely speak. I finally rolled into work one day, and she was really mad...like, really mad, ha! She said, "Why haven't you gone to the doctor yet?" "Well, I don't really have a doctor up here but

I think I'm ok." "You're not ok, I've called a doctor and he's going to see you right away." So I mumbled something under my breath, ha, and she reprimanded me for "Sassing" her and said "Go!" I made a smart decision, based on the fact that I need money in the future, and in an effort to keep my job, I would go to the doctor. Upon arriving, I was immediately taken to get an X-Ray and sat in a room. An older doctor came in the room, literally slammed a manila folder down on a stool, and yelled at me… this old man yelled at me, Y'all. I remember like it was yesterday, ha! "Are you stupid!?" "No sir, I don't think so?" "Don't sir me, stupid!" "Ok sir." …Because I had a smidgen of an attitude. That comment didn't really please him. Keep in mind that I've probably never been treated like this in my life. I graduated with fifty-three classmates in High School. My first science class at the U of A had more students in it than K-12 in our whole school back home. So college was a major adjustment by itself. Now I'm getting yelled at and name called by a doctor I've never met. As yelling ensued, he throws an X-Ray film up on an old school looking light box thing and said "Look at this! Can you not see this?" "Actually, No Sir, I can't… I don't really know what I'm looking at." "Those! Those are your lungs! Full of pneumonia!" "Lungs? As in plural?" I asked. "Yes, double pneumonia! Do you realize you are a few days away from actually dying? What are you thinking? Were you just going to lay around and wait to die?" "Like real death?" I asked again. It was a real question, ha! I wasn't trying to be smart about it. I guess he thought I was. He grunted and walked out of the room, slammed the door, and came back a few minutes later with a paper sack full of samples of some forms of medication and a note to excuse my classes. He said "here take all of these…one a day, and sleep. Don't ever do this again." You know I walked out of there happy, but scratching my head. "What in the world just happened in there?" I finally got better and went on with life. I got sick again a month or two later. I asked if Connie could call that doctor again to get me an appointment. Any man that scolds me into better health is worth seeing again. She said "Oh you didn't hear? He passed away not long ago." "What in the world for?" She said, "Well apparently he had some sickness and he wasn't taking care of himself." Imagine that. True Story. All of that being said, I guess it's safe to say Connie once saved my life, ha! I'm forever grateful!

I truly hope that one day Connie realizes the lives that she's touched over the years in many ways. Like all of the good ones, I don't think they realize how much of an impact they make on people. Truly inspirational people. Some even may think they aren't good enough to make such an impact. Connie needs to know. I know she's been through a lot in her life and God Bless her for it. But through all of her trials, she just keeps getting up and going...pushing through. What's crazy is although she may feel defeated inside, she has a lot more power than she thinks. People see her toughness and in reality, God continues to use her and I can truly look at her and know that she's never been defeated...and never will be.

Later in my freshman year we had to work color guard auditions. To spare you a bunch of details, during the process, I noticed a cute little blonde and tried to introduce myself. She was not shy. I remember that much. Full on conversation within minutes. She was still a senior in high school but auditioning to come to U of A the next year. Like 99.7% of the people that meet me after I introduce myself, it's like some weird mental block where they say "No he didn't say Hutch, he had to have said Butch." So honestly, she called me "Butch" the whole day…but I was totally ok with it, ha! At the end of the day, I didn't know if she made color guard or not, but she did make an impact on me. I went to run an errand, and when I came back, she was gone…forever. I knew her name was Meghan and that was about it. I was bummed, but at the time it was the story of my life. As the next year rolled around and new students were coming and getting checked in, I looked for her name on the color guard roster and didn't see a "Meghan." I was slightly crushed but I went on about my day. On the second day of check in I noticed her from a distance and I knew then that I couldn't let her get away. I know that sounds creepy, and that's totally not how I just wrote that, ha! So I tried to win her over. I didn't have much money, but I was a heck of a golfer at the time and could putt lights out. I had won three free games of putt-putt at the local course. To get her to go out with me for the first time, I pretty much had to take her and two other girls out at the same time. Some would call that awesome…and it was, however, I only had interest in one and to win her I had to win the others over…so I thought. So, with seven dollars and three free putt-putt games in my pocket, I somehow managed to take three girls to sonic for drinks and get four games of putt-putt. She had a problem with her car later that night and after we dropped the other two off I went to help her fix the car on a speaker call with her dad, of all people, who seemed a little freaked out that his daughter was with a random stranger, but in the end, it all worked out… We were together through college and married in the summer of 2004. She's strong and she keeps me on my toes. I like to act all tough around her, but she knows I can't make it without her. If she doesn't know, well she does now. I have the best wife, ever.

College life lead us to a multitude of lifelong friends. If I tried to name them all right now, I'd leave someone out and that would crush me. But they know who they are, and they know we love them. Every single friend we made had roles in my life's story and this whole predicament I would one day be in. When people tell you that you can't do things, don't listen to them. How different would my life be if I had taken the somewhat easier road of community college? It's obvious God had other plans and somehow by His Grace I was able to stay the course.

During college my dad met a lady through a mutual friend in ministry. Her name was Stacey. Nothing at all against short people. Stacey was barely four and a half feet tall...in heels. On the outward, my dad, older in age and "country," if you will, who owns twenty eight and a half shirts but only seems to wear seven of them... somehow defied the laws of nature and convinced this firecracker of a personality, whose spunky, city girl personality exploded pure joy every time she walked into a room, well, he convinced her to marry him. Actually, she would have been the first to say that she actually convinced him to marry her. Regardless, you didn't argue with her. She owned a purse, necklace, ear ring, and pair of shoes for every day of the year. She was New York with a hint of Texas... and proud of it.

Stacey was older than us, but she was definitely closer to our age than Dad is. We gave her heck. I hope she enjoyed it. We bonded, but we also took the small age gap to chip away at her with little jokes and that made for a fun time. When they got married she moved in to the house we grew up in. I mean, that's my house. Even if I'm married, I'll walk right up to the door right now and walk in. I just don't think too much of it and Dad is always there to welcome me. That was a struggle for her and rightfully so. But Dad was quick to remind her that she married a guy with kids and they'd always have a place in his home.

She would strive to be proper. We didn't. I remember one visit from college I came in and I was thirsty. Out of habit, I just reached in a cabinet and found the first thing I could drink out of. Apparently, I grabbed a measuring cup and proceeded to fill it full of ice and cola. She was livid. I found it hilarious as she looked up at me and tried to inform me that I couldn't drink from that. Thinking she was joking I just grinned and took another sip. I guess she wasn't joking. She told on me, Ha! Dad calmed her down and started picking at her, making her laugh, and it became a running joke between us. Honestly, I did what I could to pester her and she knew it. I guess it was my subconscious way of showing her my approval.

Stacey loved the Lord. It was apparent. I had never met someone who was so animated about it either. Her faith was stronger than I've ever seen. Nothing scared her. She had a rough childhood. She had everything stacked against her and still, she kept loving God and just spent a lifetime thankful for her every breath. But most of all, Dad loved her and she loved him and I was glad he was able to have that joy back in his life.

Stacey was a lifelong diabetic. Her diabetes was some of the worst I had ever seen, but she managed it very well. She had taken a stumble down a flight of stairs and fractured her foot. She didn't realize it. After some time, it had become infected and with her illness, even at such a young age, she had to have her leg amputated. I remember Dad taking her to UAMS in Little Rock. When they got home, Dad looked at me and said "I've never met someone who has so much joy about the news of having her leg amputated." She had done extensive research on the subject. She knew if the doctor could save ten centimeters down from her knee that she'd be able to have a prosthetic. He said she was so excited when the doctor told her he would be able to leave her those ten centimeters. Her words? "Praise God, I'm so excited! He is so good. Even through all of this, I'm still going to be able to walk!" Dad said, "Son I've learned a lot from her. I would have been devastated, yet she found joy in any way she could." That's just who Stacey was.

Shortly after the surgery, some of Stacey's close college friends wanted to come have a girls night. Stacey was still recovering but she was excited to have them in. To ensure they had a complete "girls night out" time, Dad rented them a single room at the local motel. Apparently they had a blast. Stacey had been given a new form of insulin after her amputation surgery that was not only fast acting, but more powerful. We don't exactly know what happened, but I happened to be in town visiting at the time. Dad ran into my room and woke me around five or six in the morning. One of Stacey's friends had called and said she wasn't responding. From what we could make of it, they said she had fallen asleep and started snoring before anyone else. She had taken her insulin and they just assumed she was tuckered out. They said it sounded like she was snoring and they felt sorry for her and kind of laughed it off as her just having talked and had herself a time. They didn't realize she had fallen into diabetic shock. They woke up hours later to find her still in the same position, still snoring, came to a realization that it may not be snoring, and they called my dad. We rushed to the hotel and Dad knew it wasn't good. We called an ambulance and while waiting Dad checked her sugar. It was six. Like, literally the number six. It wasn't anyone's fault. It just happened. He looked over at the nightstand and she always had a cola in case she had a low. He said "She's too good at this to not realize she was getting this low." The cola was unopened. So we knew it had to be a result of her not fully understanding the doses of that new insulin. The ambulance arrived and they wheeled her to the back of the ambulance. I stayed with her and she was still unconscious. The EMT said he needed to get her levels up so he started an IV, grabbed a huge syringe of what appeared to be glucagon and he shot that whole tube in her within a half second. I don't know if it was supposed to happen like that, but when he did, she immediately sat up on the gurney, still unconscious, and started having a seizure. They closed the doors and rushed her to the hospital. She ended up in a coma with little brain activity so they flew her to UAMS.

I didn't want to leave Dad. I could see the heartbreak in his eyes every day. She was in ICU and they would let us go back and see her for short periods of time. He would sit there and pray for her, sing to her, talk to her... it took everything I had to hold it together. They didn't know if she would wake up. I can't remember how long she was out but I know it was longer than a week. Eventually they would only let one of us go back to see her at a time. We'd sleep in the waiting room of the ICU and when available, family and church friends would reserve Dad a room at a nearby motel so he could rest. I wanted to hold out hope for him, but I didn't have much at the time. I didn't know how all of it worked but I didn't think it was going to end well. I kept a brave face for him.

One evening it was time for visiting hours to start back so I went back to check on her. Dad was talking to a visitor so I took the opportunity to go back. We were instructed to talk to her as much as we could just to see if we could stimulate something. When I made it to her room I could see her eyes were open. They were slightly fixed and at first it frightened me. I ran into the room and when I did she looked over at me. I lost it. I couldn't believe she was awake! I informed the nurse and he started to come in. She looked puzzled. She didn't recognize me. I remember thinking, "She doesn't have a clue who I am." I didn't care, I was just glad she was awake. I didn't know what to do. I looked at her and said "Stacey!" It was like a light clicked, she grabbed my arm, almost as if angry, and said "I need your dad!" I ran out of that room and grabbed Dad. I ran Y'all... down the hall and I feel bad because Dad thought something bad had happened. He saw me crying and running. I just screamed "She's Awake." I remember all of our new friends in the ICU waiting room who had been with us waiting for their loved ones to recover were overjoyed. Some were shouting. Some were crying tears of joy. It was a special moment. I saw my Uncle Tommy cry for the first time, and I saw my dad run for the first time in my life. He ran, Y'all. If Y'all know him like I know him... he doesn't run, Ha! I tried to trail him but I just let him go. I was so relieved for both her and him.

Stacey wasn't out of the woods yet. She had a lot of recovering to do. She had to learn to do a lot of things over again and honestly, she'd know you one minute, and not know you the next. I had never seen anything like it. It was heartbreaking at times. It had only been a few weeks since she'd had her leg amputated. So short term memory was the last thing to come back. I remember she would sit up in bed, look down where her leg should be, feel for it, and notice it was gone. Tears would well up in her eyes and she'd just sit there with her mouth wide open…astonished. She'd put her hand over her mouth, and it was like the shock of the surprise would cause her to pass out. She would fall back on the bed and be asleep. An hour later, Y'all she would wake up, notice it all over again, and repeat. It was one of the saddest things I've ever seen. Doctors said it was normal. I complained, but they assured me. Later they moved her from ICU to a regular room. Dad and I took turns sleeping in there with her. Dad was completely worn down. So I did my best to do as much as I could for him. They couldn't restrain her. But she didn't realize what was going on. So we practically had to stay up all night with her because as she started regaining certain things, she would try to get more independent. She had no business being independent. But you couldn't tell her that. Plus she still didn't remember having her leg amputated. That made things very scary. One night I woke up and she had climbed on the side of the bed. I literally got up in time to catch her as she was falling to the floor. She was trying to walk to the bathroom. I said "Stacey you can't do that! Please!" She got so mad at me. She said, "Cliff Preston! You can't tell me what to do!" I said, "Well good because I'm Hutch but close enough! Now get back in bed." That made her more frustrated. But it was all such a long road of learning.

She graduated to a rehab facility where she had to be taught simple things. Simple words that we take for granted. How to get dressed again. How to brush her teeth again. What a toothbrush even is. Once it started to come back, it seemed to come back pretty quick. She was finally able to come home but she still wasn't a hundred percent. I don't know that she ever fully gained all of that back. I do remember when she got home, I reached into the cabinet and found an old measuring cup. I filled it with ice. She couldn't talk but she started trying to scream to Dad to tell on me. I knew when that happened she was doing better.

In the process of the coma they had to perform a tracheotomy. It was really sad. She was famous for her singing but now she was limited to what she could make through the instrument that helped her breathe. From that point on, she got around ok, but you could tell her body was just wearing down from all of the stress. She would always say, "I've lived a great life and when God calls me home, no matter when it is, I'm ready!" You could tell she actually meant it. That was the special thing about it. One morning around seven o'clock she hit my dad on the leg in the bed. He said she was having trouble breathing and was visibly shaken. This wasn't totally uncommon because sometimes her trach would get clogged and they'd have to perform some kind of suction procedure to free the airway. He asked her if she needed suction and she nodded yes. He ran into the kitchen to grab the kit and by the time he got back to her, she was gone. Her trach was fine, but her heart had given out on her. I know Dad was, and still is devastated.

We all hated to lose Stacey but we know she was ready when God called her home. I hated to see Dad go through losing someone again. We all do our best to encourage him. Her loss has taken a huge toll on him. But, even in her loss, he still remains faithful and I have so much admiration for him from that.

Stacey was a special person. We had many talks about faith and she ministered to me more than she will ever know. I feel like I was able to bond with her even more through that time and losing her bothered me even more than I ever thought it would. But when I doubted my faith, she was the one there to pick me up. I remember her praying with me one day that God would restore that faith, and I'm forever grateful for that. There are a lot of special people in our lives and those that have played special parts in my own. Stacey was one of them. I needed to tell her story and you'll know why later. But I thank God that he brought her into our lives... even if just for a short time.

# 4

## MY HIDDEN BATTLE

I need to share this part of my life with you as well. As I mentioned earlier, I struggle tremendously with Panic Disorder accompanied with Agoraphobia. Again, it almost offends me to hear someone say they had a panic attack because of something that randomly happens to them, seemingly over it in only a few minutes. Example, "I lost my wallet, and I just about had a panic attack." Well, losing your wallet would probably cause you some anxiety, but I'm not talking about normal every day anxiety. A true panic attack is crippling. Not to discredit anyone's anxiety. I get it. It's no fun. But when you deal with actual Panic Disorder, you don't just shrug it off and take a pill. You try to go find help. You are absolutely desperate for help. Then there are times where your "help" doesn't seem to help. You learn about certain triggers that may spark these things. That's where the Agoraphobia comes in. To me, feeling trapped in any situation seems like a death sentence. You create an internal, subconscious need to be in control of your situation at all times. Now, prolonged anxiety can trigger a panic attack... which is why you rarely see me NOT driving my own vehicle when I go places. If I go on trips with friends or family, it says a lot if I actually let you drive. It's not anything against you, but the anxiety I have of actually not being in control of that vehicle is overwhelming. If I do let you drive, I'm probably still in the front seat. I don't know why it's comfortable for me, and it's actually still not comfortable, but it at least gives me a little more security than being in the back seat or three rows back on a bus or van. That's a nightmare for me. If I'm going with a group of people to a location, I like to have my own vehicle. What if I need to leave? What if I need to get away? Now, over the years, I've learned that I can talk myself out of certain feelings and anxieties. Sometimes it gets pretty outrageous but whatever works, you know? I'm not crazy. Sometimes I think I am, Ha! But it's a true disorder and it's something that I just have to deal with. Currently, I'm fortunate to have a great support staff in my life that has been there for me and I have been able to get a good grip on these attacks and pretty much been able to eliminate them from my life, for the most part.

I remember as a child having them and not knowing what they were. My parents had no clue and back then, no one really knew enough about it to do anything. Many times I would actually get in trouble for "acting out," or just completely losing it. I don't blame my parents...we just didn't know. Anything that can disrupt my "normal" has potential to trigger this disorder. Mainly situations that I can't get out of or feel like I can't get out of. Permanent things. Absolutes. Huge life changes. I would often spend the night at a friend's house and call to come home. My stomach would start turning and I'd get nauseated. By the time I got home, I was fine. It was normal again. I hated it. Y'all are going to think this is nuts, but we walked home from school every day…and when it rained, I couldn't walk home in the rain. We would have to wait for my dad to come pick us up. He never forgot about us. But when it rained on a school day during elementary school, my stomach would be in knots all day. What if dad forgot to pick us up? What would we do? The fear I had was being there alone, afraid the teachers, students, and everyone else would leave and I'd be there waiting for my dad to come and have no way out of the situation. What IS crazy is how irrational that is. The older I got, the easier it was to rationalize those situations…thank goodness. But those situations also manifested in seemingly "updated" versions of irrationalities. Man, Y'all are never going to want to hang out with me, Ha! But you need to know this. I'm fine, I promise!

It explains my personality. I'm horrible at first impressions. When I first meet you, or if I'm in a group of people that I don't know for the first time, I'm mentally circling like a buzzard. Not to devour you, but mainly to figure you out. Again, I'm not judging you. I just need to know how you're going to respond to things. This makes me appear to be stuck up or snotty. I'm not. Some have even said that I'm intimidating. I could see that, I guess. A heavy, bearded guy who doesn't speak and socially keeps to himself at first glance… I could totally see that. That's really not me, though. I just have to at least think that I have you figured out and once I'm comfortable around you, I'll loosen up. Boy do I loosen up! But getting to that point is full of gut wrenching anxiety. By this time in my life, I'm good at it, and you probably don't notice…I hope. Give me time, I'll open up. If I never open up, for some reason, I'm not comfortable around you. Don't take it personal. Having said that, one of the biggest downfalls of this is I've become very successful at catching personalities almost immediately and frankly, like anyone, there are some personalities that I don't mix well with. I have about a ninety percent success rate. The problem with this is that leftover ten percent where I'm actually wrong. It could be for good, or for bad. I've most likely missed out on some great friendships. I've also steered away from people only to find out years later that they're not so bad after all. On the flip side, I've probably saved myself from some serious heartache as well. If I do open up and you win me over...congrats! You have a lifelong friend! If I become comfortable around you, I'm loyal to a fault. Because I value having friends and a support system so much, I tend to cling to those relationships and I never want to let go. I'm not constantly hovering over you like a creepy boyfriend or girlfriend, but just know that there is no value that can be placed on our friendship. Having said that, if the friendship is damaged for any reason, I'm completely heartbroken. No matter whose fault it is, for me to feel like I've lost a friendship is completely devastating. I will dwell on it for days and even years. It will consume me. So for all of those reasons, my life is full of a constant need to be "on guard" and studying every scenario that I may be faced with daily for a way in or out if I need one. I've always said I would be a good risk assessor for a large company. I know the irony of that being I should have seen an accident coming, but it's not that easy. Most of the time I will break down every scenario to find every possible negative situation that could come from it, and try to avoid it...or at least be prepared for it. I can get pretty creative. If I'm not careful, I will take the worst case scenario and dwell on it. When I dwell on that worst case scenario, that's where the panic triggers lie. So yes, when I ride in the car with you, and I'm not driving, my mind is constantly racing and the only thing I can think about is you hitting a tree, and if I were driving, I could at least prevent that. Yes, because of this, I will talk myself out of situations so I won't even have to participate...and I hate that.

I spend a ton of time performing what's known as "cognitive therapy." So when you have a panic attack, one thing that is for certain is if you actually suffer from the disorder, you absolutely live in fear of having another. As I said before, you can trigger one just by being so afraid that you will have one...you actually give yourself one. While experiencing these attacks, your body does certain things. Your heart races. You sweat. Your stomach turns and you get nauseated. You can have difficulty breathing. I tend to get this warm, flushed sensation. A fight or flight response. They don't last long, but they can repeat themselves all day long. The more I had them the more I would associate those feelings and bodily changes with panic attacks. The problem is those bodily changes can happen and it may not even involve a panic attack at all...but the feeling of such change can trigger an attack. I use the cognitive therapy to basically change the way I think and essentially I talk myself out of attacks. Although not always possible, it does tend to work the majority of the time. I avoid foods that will make my stomach mimic the feeling of a panic attack. If I do feel an attack may have been triggered, I can convince myself by saying "Hey, you just ate _____, that's why your stomach feels that way...this is not an attack. You're fine." That typically works.

Huge life changes can bring them on as well. I

remember when I really started to struggle with them was when Dave went to college. I had experienced them before, but when he left, the major life change really sent me for a loop. It shouldn't have. That's what's so confusing, but it did. I don't know how it works. I just know that when he was gone, things were different. Change was no good. It was a highly stressful time for me and again, it shouldn't have been, but it was.

Even short term changes were scary for me. I think it's mainly the feeling of no way out. I remember when my parents would go out of the country for Olympic events, it would be a big deal to me. What if I needed them home as soon as possible? The fear of knowing it would take them hours if not days to get back to me would be crippling. The farther away they went, the worse it got. My Granny Preston would take care of us a lot while my parents were gone. As I've explained before, I think the proper term for her is "Spit Fire," and that may not even do her justice! We grew up on a big lot of land, and my dad still lives on that eleven or so acres that she owns and it happens to be the same farm area where Dad grew up as a child. She is very attached to that land. When Mom and Dad went out of town, for anything, it became a work day and she automatically got three, well-kept young men to help her do whatever she wanted to said land. "Don't sass me," was a common phrase heard from her mouth and honestly, I didn't really know what "sassing" was but I'm pretty sure we never did it…it sounded horrible and the way she said it came across as if there were huge repercussions. If we denied "sassing," for some reason that was actually considered sassing? Still not really sure on that one. We just know that when she said it, we just said "Yes, Ma'am," and moved along…quickly. We worked in a huge garden growing vegetables. The woman loved tomatoes. So eighty percent of our garden was tomatoes, or so it seemed. The rest was some form of pea. It didn't really matter the species…as long as it was able to be shelled and you had to employ your grandkids to sit on your front porch and shell them until their fingers turned blue. I don't even know why I say "employed," as if we were getting paid…yeah right.

I remember the time when my parents went to Russia for the Goodwill Games. They actually took Dave with them and that left Cliff and me at home. Granny Preston had a number of chores for us to do. She just wanted the place to look good when my dad got home. I remember struggling with this trip pretty bad. The older I got and still didn't understand what was going on, the worse the attacks got. I was old enough to realize that this wasn't normal…at all. But I didn't know how to stop it. That made it worse. I would pray, I would scream, I would cry…nothing. It was terrifying. I remember one of the days while they were gone she had us working in the yard. I was on a big lawn tractor hauling away. I cried the whole time. I was just in fear of everything. I literally thought I was going crazy. I'm a young teenager here. Riding on a tractor and bawling my eyes out. I was scared of her and what she might do if she saw me crying. So as I took a loop and started back towards her where she was working, I'd dry my face up, pull my hat down and move forward. I'd be able to hold it together long enough to make it past her and then as I drove away, I'd let go again. It was so bad that as I would get down to the end of the lane I was cutting, I'd just let out a huge scream into the woods and let out the frustration. Finally a few loops back she stopped me and asked why in the world I was crying and "hollering" as she called it. I wasn't hollering. I told her I didn't know what was wrong. I just wanted it to stop. She wasn't mad and I don't want you to think she was mean. But at the time, she was the only adult security that I had to hold on to and if she was angry with me, then my mind would feel as if I was alone. There was this weird feeling that as long as she was around and ok, then I'd be ok. At the moment she may turn on me, all bets were off. So I think that's the reason I tried to shield it from her. Understand that absolutely none of us, including parents, brothers, sisters…no one knew what was going on. We didn't know it was actually a medical disorder. I can't imagine being in their shoes at the time. They probably felt as helpless as I did.

As with any panic attack, they are only temporary. I finally calmed down and she did ok helping with that. But I did live in fear of having another one and that whole time my parents were gone, I just kept having them. Most of them were now triggered by the fear of having another. Once they got home, everything was back to normal and I was fine. I know my grandma mentioned it to Dad and we talked about it. He was concerned but neither of us knew what it was or how to stop it. I was fine until Dave left a few weeks later for college and then it hit again and for a very long time. At that point, it became a regular part of my life. My mind dwelled on what happened while they were at Russia and that life change messed up my normal again. It was like a vicious, unrelenting cycle.

During that Russia trip, my Aunt Linda had to take us somewhere and we stayed with her until my Grandma could come and get us. She took us to get fast food and knowing what I know now about food and how it can trigger attacks, the place we ate at is full of the things that commonly trigger those attacks. Again, we had no clue. So later that evening I felt sick to my stomach and sure enough it started an attack. Cliff looked at me in the face and he just went and got her. I was trying so hard to get it to go away. She was actually really calm and reassuring. That really helped. The fear that someone would lash out at me for having one was constantly hovering over me. To know that someone at least acted like they understood and cared, really did comfort me. It's not that Granny Preston didn't care, I think she just didn't understand it and the only proper way she knew how to handle it was to resort back to her nursing days and handle it with sternness. She wasn't mean to her patients, but she retired from a hospital and her floor mainly handled people who were addicted to substances. I mean, we're talking about the lady who when I was eighteen and had my tonsils removed, only let me have a half of a pain pill a day because she didn't want me to get addicted like the people she had to treat every day. That was miserable, by the way. So, obviously, there were many times in her career where she had to be stern about certain things. I think she just did the best she could do with what she had.

On the flip side, that's probably why I adjusted well around my other Grandma Hutcheson. They are polar opposites. Not that one is any more important than the other. I love them both dearly. But to compare them isn't even fair due to their stark differences. Granny Preston was more like "Boy, get over there and cut that tree down like I told you" while Mamaw Hutcheson would say, "Why do you have an axe! Charles! (My Grandpa) Hutch has an axe and he's going to hurt himself!" See…polar opposites. So after a week of hard labor, it was kind of a welcomed treat to sit under a cloud of pillows and be wrapped head to toe in bubble wrap at my Grandma Hutcheson's. That would probably explain why my attacks seemed to not be as prevalent there. Most of the time we spent playing with our cousin Rachel and had a great time. That definitely took my mind off of things.

I'm sure by now most of you either think I'm crazy, or well, I don't know what you think. But, I need to be vulnerable here because I want you to understand what and how I think. I encourage you to research the disorder. Maybe you know someone who suffers. One of the best things you can do for someone who suffers from this illness is be knowledgeable about it. Teach them and help comfort them through it. The more you learn about the illness, the more you can come to grips with it, how it works, why your body feels this way, and how you can fix it. I could go on and on about this but at some point I feel like I keep digging myself into a hole and you may start to worry for my safety, Ha! Some of you probably think I should pray about it, and I do…a lot. But just like any illness, God chooses to heal in many ways. I don't like it. But every day that I go without an attack, I thank God for giving me the strength to fight them off. Having this disorder shows me how tough I am. It shows me how strong God is. "He gave it to you!" No, He allows me to endure it and gives me strength to defeat it. It's one of the scariest things I can go through, but the confidence it gives me every time I defeat it, it is incomparable. If I can defeat this, I can do anything. Does the enemy use it against me? He tries. He really tries. Sometimes it's effective. As you'll see as you keep reading, he tries a lot. But it's just one more thing in my life that I can use to show God's love for me and how He gives me strength to make it through. Sometimes God gives me people to help make it through as well…

So, our dad is a huge sports fan. He loves his Arkansas Razorbacks. He coached little league baseball for years even before we were old enough to play. Naturally, he coached us as well when it was our turn. Dad has a heart for children and wanted every child to be involved if they chose. There was one kid named Wayne who was a pretty good athlete. I'm not going to go into Wayne's background and story. That's his story and not that it was horrific, but if he wants to tell it one day that's up to him. From what I remember, the only way Wayne would be able to play ball is if he had a ride to and from practice and games. Wayne played for a different team than my dad coached and Dave played on, but Dad faithfully gave him rides to and from games and practices. I remember it was nothing to have a truck full of dirty ball players with us all riding in the back of that old truck as he picked up and took every one of them home. Wayne was special and he and Dave became close friends. Dad had a heart for Wayne and his story and took him under his wing like a son. Wayne ended up moving less than a block from us and we could practically shout at him from our house. He was always over. He would spend the night, eat, play, and before long, he practically became one of us. To this day he calls my dad "Dad" and my mom "Mom." When Dad and Mom went through their issues, it effected Wayne just as much as it did all of us. We had a lot of close friends growing up. But, because Wayne practically lived with us, and because he developed a bond with my parents and associated them as his parents, he understood our family hurt as well as our family joy. He laughed when we laughed and cried when we cried. In my family's eyes, even to this day, he is one of us.

Wayne played a little football at a local college then took a good job close to home. That helped. When Dave left for college, it did help having Wayne around to partially fill that void. He didn't live with us then, but was frequently around when needed. I remember once there was a huge ice storm and where we live, we are in no way prepared for anything "ice" related…at all. If there is an inch of snow on the ground…school is probably canceled for three days. That may sound crazy to some of you, but we are just not equipped with the trucks, scrapers, salt, and whatever else is needed to clean roadways in order to make life happen. That's basically because it doesn't happen enough to invest the money in to such things. This ice storm was one of the worst in memory. There was probably four inches of just straight sleet and ice that had fallen and it was as hard as a rock. You could walk out of our back door and hear trees falling one by one from the excessive weight of ice on the limbs. Whole limbs would fall and in some cases even entire trees. You could just hear them crashing down. It didn't take much for us to lose power. During that storm I remember power going out and we had a few candles to keep light. Our stove was gas burning so most of the time we would just leave those on for minimal heat. It was boring. I remember on one of those nights it was still early in the evening but dark and cold. We were bored out of our minds. With me severely struggling with panic attacks at the time, being somewhat alone in the dark with nothing to keep your mind off of things didn't go well for me when it came to fighting these things off. Suddenly, someone knocked on the door and we went to answer. It was Wayne and he had trucked through the ice with an armful of board games to play. I remember he sat them up in the middle of our living room around a big candle and we played for hours. It seemed odd with Dave not being there, but it did help me through a rough time. Wayne has always been around through those tough times and there are many where he didn't even realize how much he helped.

I do feel like it may be an odd time in this story to introduce Wayne to you, but he did play an important role in helping me through some of these dark times. As you read further, you'll see that he hasn't stopped helping. This is just one small instance where he made a difference. Y'all, you can ask both of my natural brothers and they will tell you that Wayne is one of the hardest working men that we know. Wayne has an amazing story and statistics show that most children that were in the situation he was in, quite honestly, circle themselves back around and live their adult lives in that same situation. Wayne found a way to defeat those odds. To this day if I cook in his house, he's right behind me with a rag wiping the counter down. I don't take it personal. I just give him a hard time and say, "Bro, you know that's just going to get dirty again in a minute." He usually just laughs and moves on. One day I gave him a hard time and he just finally said, "Man I'm sorry, I can't help it. I always told myself that if I'm ever lucky enough to have something this nice one day, that I won't ever lose my appreciation for it." Woah. So I let Wayne do his thing. Over the years he has worked hard with a great job and found an even better one. He's almost worked his way to the top with the company he is with and it's so awesome to see someone work so hard. I'm so proud of him. He has a wife Kristie and a son Austen. Austen is about eight feet eleven inches tall...just kidding. But he's huge. I've literally watched him raise Austen from diapers and maybe he doesn't see it himself, but I see my dad in Wayne and how he raises his son every day. I'm so glad to be able to share my dad with Wayne. I hope he knows how much we love him.

# 5

# MORE THAN AN ACCIDENT

It's finally that moment. I have many events that I long for each year. But this week is special. I take a week and spend it in Smackover with my family. Hanging around the deer camp. Cooking BBQ and telling stories. Joking with people who miss deer (mainly us) and overall fellowship. But, most of all, we laugh. It's a fun week and there is nothing like it. The week leading up is like slow motion. I work as much as I can to load up, pack, get things together and be ready to drive away as soon as possible. Typically I take about eleven days and it starts on the Thursday before the opening Saturday. I pack the remainder of my gear up on Thursday morning and start the 5 hour drive down. On Friday, we do some last minute preparing on our hunting spots and get a good rest for the morning. Thursdays are typically fun. A little stressful but once I get on the road I'm all smiles. I have goose bumps riding down the whole way. I'm laughing, waving at everyone, screaming to the radio and seeing if I can make it without stopping to go to the bathroom. In my younger years I was pretty successful, however, those dreams of making it all the way now vanish around Clarksville...an hour and fifteen minutes into my trip. With that being said, for some reason, this year was different. Something was off.

I had a stressful day on Thursday. I was looking forward to deer season but I just wasn't as excited as I usually was. I was trying to leave early so I could catch a Smackover football game being played that night. Dave was an assistant coach and they were playing a night early to accommodate for playoffs. I wanted to catch a game before the season was over. On the way home I was miserable. To this day, I can't pin point the reason why, other than I was so emotionally gone that I couldn't think straight. I think I cried the whole way home. I was scared. For some reason I had this pit in my stomach. I truly thought I was going to die. From Alma to Conway my mind was overflowing with ways I could die in a hunting accident. That's only if I made it there because a car accident could happen at any moment. I can remember white knuckling the steering wheel at ten and two, tears rolling down my cheeks and I was doing about ten miles per hour under the speed limit, staring at the road waiting for something to happen. As for hunting, I kept imagining my gun going off at the wrong time. Coincidentally, the deer stand that I normally hunted on wasn't in great shape and we were stressed about whether it would hold up another year...especially with this tiny beast of myself climbing in it. We didn't have time to prepare anything else so it was going to have to work. I was a wreck. By the time I made it through Little Rock I was only about two hours away. I had just experienced roughly three hours of complete torment. Not that the thought of dying was unheard of in my life over the last few months. This time, I knew something was up. I just couldn't get my hand on it. I started praying. I didn't even know what I was praying. My spiritual self-worth was so low. I really didn't think God would even care. I know it sounds crazy coming from someone who should know better, but I wasn't thinking clearly. I can assure you, there is a time where you can work yourself so far away from God that nothing seems to be right anymore. Nothing works. Nothing rhymes. Nothing makes sense. "Loose cannon" becomes a huge understatement. I was there and I didn't even realize it. I continued praying, this time praying that God would let me live. I didn't want to die. "God please don't let me die," I would keep saying over and over. It was one of the worst feelings I have had to date. I continued to drive on. As I got closer, the worry turned into a reality. I was convinced something would happen...I just didn't know when. I even had this "it's your own fault," thing going on. Ironically it kind of calmed me down. I had made peace with going on.

I finally made it and immediately got into the car with Cliff to travel to the football game. Dad was already on his way and we were running a little late. I don't remember much about the ride there. I do remember getting out at this place, excusing my quietness as just being tired. We made our way around to the visitors section. I told Cliff I just wanted to stand the whole game on the fence. He said "you don't want to go up and sit down?" I didn't. If I went up there I'd have to talk to people and I didn't want to do that. I couldn't process life at the moment, much less worrying about being nice. At the state I was in, surely people would notice something wasn't right. So we stood there and watched the remainder of the game. I could see my dad sitting in the bleachers. It was his birthday but I didn't even have the nerve to walk over and tell him Happy

Birthday. The game ended and we had about a two hour drive back to Smackover. We couldn't find a place to eat so we stopped at a gas station and grabbed a few snacks. I was short tempered and Cliff had just driven in from Nashville, TN so we were both tired and cranky. We drove on home made some small talk about the work we needed to do the next day and went home to bed.

The next morning I woke up and was a little more excited than I was the day before. But something still wasn't right. I got up and tried to find a little breakfast and my dad came into the kitchen with me. I could tell he was a little down too. He asked if I was ok and I told him I didn't know. "Dad something's just not right this year...I'm just not excited about it like I always am." He made mention that he was a little down too but wanted to make the best of it. "Let's just go enjoy it and forget about everything...be happy." I agreed and it seemed to work. After all I was doing what I loved and we had a lot of work to do and we didn't have time to worry about things. We hopped in the truck and made our way out to the lease.

My Uncle Larry, Dad's brother, owns a brush hog. Every year he gives up a little time to come out and mow a couple of lanes for us. Water was a little high and it was hard to get us all together until that week. Most of the time our work is done last minute. Even mowing, which some think is crazy, but we always see deer. We went to my deer stand and it didn't need much work. Just the usual mowing of a couple of lanes and we really needed to check the sturdiness of my deer stand. Before mowing my Uncle Larry climbed up into it and jumped around a bit. It stands pretty tall so it's a hefty fall if it decided to go down. I stood at the bottom prepared to catch him. I would probably act more as a landing pad than a catcher but I was ready anyway. It rocked and swayed some but he deemed it acceptable and reluctantly I did too. I didn't climb into it and took him at his word. I was already trying to work out an alternate spot because I didn't want to climb in that thing and I was convinced if I did right then, it would come down and that'd be it. He finished mowing the lanes and the last cut he backed into the area next to the stand to mow a small spot where I could walk in. There was a piece of old plastic tubing about 5 feet in length laying on the ground. I remember seeing him back into that spot and the back wheel of his tractor sunk in and it caused it and the brush hog to tilt slightly. I could see the blade spinning and remember thinking how dangerous that is. At that time the brush hog shot out that plastic pipe and it flew in my direction. It landed a few feet from me and it made me think if I were closer how it could have just snapped my legs in two. Crazy. I took a few steps back, laughed it off and took a look at my dad who was standing off to the side. He made this crazy "that was close" face and we went on about our business. Looking back, it's almost disturbing how things happen. Almost like a warning that you can't interpret.

After we left my hunting spot we had accomplished everything on our list for the day. Dad suggested we go and get some lunch then head to our camp to see if anyone was around that we could talk to. I also needed to drop off my smoker for cooking during the week. We went by the local gas station and grabbed a burger and drink and made it out to the camp. We saw Bob and he asked how everything was going. I got out to unhook the smoker as Bob brought up Cliff's hunting spot.

Cliff hunts on the edge of a clear cut. We have quite a bit of land to hunt on. Most of the land is owned by timber companies and we just lease hunting rights from them. From time to time, they will come and clear the land, cutting down all of the trees and selling them to sawmills. When they cut an area, they take time to let the leftover tree tops and brush die, then they come in and spray the area with a chemical that speeds that up. Once everything is officially clear, they come back through and replant trees, wait until the trees mature and start the process all over again. Cliff's area was about on year 6 of that process. The replanted trees were tall enough that we could actually spot them over or through the tall sage grass that tends to grow in these clearings. The deer love to bed up in those areas. This deer stand was placed on the edge of that clearing right on the property line. Deer would cross from the clear cut in the morning into the other property with an abundance of hardwood growth to feed. In the evenings, they would make their way back across.

Over the years it gets harder and harder to see. The taller the grass and new trees grow, the more the deer are concealed while crossing the line. We were not allowed to mow the area because the timber company was afraid we would accidentally cut down their new trees. When talking to Bob at the camp, he informed us that the clear cut land had changed hands in ownership. There are a couple of oil pumps on the property and the owner of those pumps was tired of not being allowed to mow the property either, so he just purchased the land from the timber company. Our camp had since made a verbal lease with him to hunt the land exclusively. That being said, Bob informed us that we could now mow Cliff a strip down that property line to better see the crossing. Although we were already done for the day, this was big news as we knew this would increase the success at this spot. We called my Uncle and made our way back out to the lease and down to Cliff's spot. Cliff, who was conveniently running late all day, had luckily missed out on every bit of work we did due to some errands he was running. I called him to let him know we were going to work on his area and the least he could do was come out and watch. I was slightly bitter but the main thing was getting it done. I was riding with Dad in our old truck and he had just received a phone call from a client of his. I finished my burger and drink as he was on the phone. Uncle Larry pulled up and was ready to go, so I motioned to Dad that I was going to help guide him in and I'd see him when he got done with his phone call. As a Christian Counselor, it's normal for his phone calls to last minutes up to an hour so I was unsure about the time he would be out to help. He stayed in the truck and I went on. It's tricky to get the tractor into the area. We have to navigate through a lane that is about 10 feet wide and has a very low hanging power line that feeds electricity to a pump nearby. Driving a big tractor and dodging that thing is scary enough. We got it accomplished and made our way on to the site. The deer stand itself is only about forty yards off the main road of the lease but you can barely see it from there. It's a definite "you can't get there from here" moment because the brush has grown so high, you have to come in from the side. Even though it added another hundred or so yards of distance, coming in from the side gave us access to the power line lane and a clear shot to the deer stand itself. Once there Uncle Larry waited for me to get by him. I told him I was going to climb up into the stand and guide him down the line we needed cut. I stand right at 6 feet tall myself. There were bunches of grass that were about a foot taller than my head. The tall grass made it hard for him to see where to go and the progress he was making, so I was going to help along.

The deer stand itself was made very well by a former member of the camp. Many hunters shimmy up trees and strap themselves in, standing on a platform that's about a foot and a half in diameter. We are big guys, we don't shimmy up trees and we don't stand on platforms whose circumference is smaller than our belly, Ha! Once, a few years back, I purchased a tree stand. You know, I wanted to bow hunt and to do that I had to climb up a tree and conceal myself. So I got a tree stand that seemed sturdy. You latched the bottom section to the tree and stood on it. While standing on the bottom section, you take the top section and wrap it around you and the tree as it did its best to hold you in. To get up the tree, you sat on the top section and your weight dug its teeth into the tree. While sitting, you would grab the bottom section of the stand with your feet and jar it loose from the tree. Lifting up with your feet, you would slide the bottom section of the stand up the tree until you were in a squatting position. You would then stand up and the weight of your body would force the teeth of the bar into the tree as it wrapped around. With your arms you then grabbed the top section you were sitting on, which was now at about your knees, pulled it up to your waist and sat on it again…locking in its own section of teeth to support your weight. Repeat the process a few times and you literally shimmy up the tree. Some hunters get very high. I've heard of people that get up to thirty feet or higher. Height is key here. So I tried this. Not a fan of heights, especially when the platform is see through. I shimmied my way up the tree to a height I felt comfortable with. I really felt like I was high. I could feel the wind swaying the tree I was latched onto. In a spot where I was confident I would see a deer, I did everything right. I was down wind, did my best to cover my scent and was well camouflaged. I didn't know why I wasn't seeing any deer. After a couple of hours I decided to climb down. Confused, I ran through everything I could have possibly done wrong. Then I thought, "surely I'm high enough?" So for good measure and reference, I grabbed my pocket knife, slowly squatted down and made a notch in the tree at the bottom platform where my feet were. When I got down, I could see exactly how high I was and determine if it was sufficient. Being that I went as high as I was going to go due to fear, if this didn't meet the requirement, my tree climbing days were numbered. I shimmied down, out of breath, and unhooked both sections from the tree. True story…I stood back and took a look at my notch. Thinking I was more than twenty or so feet up the tree, at least that's what it felt like, I was astonished when I walked up and put my finger in the notch I cut. That's right, I could touch it. I really didn't even have to reach. It was just higher than eye level which means my feet were no more than six feet off the ground. Yep, I stood there in all of my glory "hunting" in plain sight. To this day I still don't see how I messed that up. Embarrassed, and slightly amused, I took the tree stand and neatly placed it back in its box and prayed the store would take it back. That! Is the reason big people like us don't climb trees. We build or find these huge boxes that are supposed to be safe and sturdy. Ninety-nine percent of the time they are. In this case, this one was built very well and made of solid wood, it should have stood another ten years or longer.

Because of my burly stature, climbing into this deer stand wasn't an easy feat, either. There are no stairs, but a slanted ladder that was built into the structure itself. I can remember climbing into it thinking, "man, I've go to lose some weight." It was harder than I wanted it to be and at the time I was seriously considering a staircase attachment but overall I made it inside and sat for a moment to catch my breath. Inside this deer stand is an old recliner that is attached to an old tire rim that may or may not be filled with concrete. None the less, it swivels on this rim as well as reclines back for comfort. It's very bulky in relation to the space you have in the stand to maneuver but in what it lacks, it makes up for in comfort. Leaves and debris had made its way into the bottom as well as a few wasp nests that were empty. I stood up to start knocking those down and sweeping debris out with my foot while Uncle Larry mowed a few close strips to free some area around the stand itself. I could feel the vibrations of the tractor and it really didn't concern me at first. I stood looking out the front waiting for him to pass and head towards the line. I couldn't see him but I did feel an increase in shaking and it made me laugh a little to myself thinking, "We can probably get the rest of the close stuff with a weed eater or something." I never felt immediately threatened, however, I made a quick decision to turn around and attempt to climb out of the stand for safety until he could get clear of the area. Just to give you an idea of what I'm faced with here, because you enter the stand from the bottom portion of the back area, there's not an upper part of the door. There is basically a twenty-four inch gap or so that stands about four feet tall. So, when you're climbing into the back of this thing and coming up, you're never in danger of hitting your head on the upper back wall. When leaving, you climb down the ladder and again, your head clears the upper back portion of the wall. When you're standing inside the deer stand and facing the back wall, you would have to duck under the two to three feet section of upper wall to even see out. Basically, my window of opportunity to get out of the box in a hurry was to squeeze out of a roughly two by three and a half foot hole. I'm not completely sure of the exact height of the stand either. I would like to say from floor to ground it was about, more or less, ten feet. Immediately looking out the back, because the grass was so tall, it didn't seem as high as it was. My weight sure didn't help matters either.

As I turned around in an effort to climb out, to this day, I'm not a hundred percent sure what exactly happened. I didn't see anything. The deer stand shook pretty well and I could tell the tractor was still close. We don't know if it was a direct hit, or if something had hit it during the off season and vibrations jarred it loose, we really don't know. All I know is I heard a loud pop that rivaled the sound of a shotgun. The deer stand slowly started to lean into a fall. As I mentioned earlier, my own deer stand was in its final days. I had always planned that if it were to ever fall, I would attempt to jump out of it rather than falling down while still inside. In my opinion, riding down on the inside would only subject myself to more injury because of split boards, nails, and just the immediate possibility of blunt force trauma to my head or body. So, in this case, instinctively, somehow I squeezed through the back of this thing and jumped before it made its way to the ground. I can tell you that it will amaze you how fast your mind will think in those situations. The thoughts that roll through your head. This isn't science here, but I can guestimate that it took me only a couple of seconds to hit the ground. Like, literally two seconds. During that time, I had the awareness to tell myself to attempt to jump as far away from this thing as possible. I was also slightly amused that it was actually coming down. So I wasn't worried about falling because it didn't feel like it was that high. I had also remembered a show I saw on television once where a guy jumped off of a house and kind of "rolled" himself down to absorb the impact. Basically, he landed on his feet at a bit of an angle and kind of flopped or rolled himself down on his side. This distributed the impact rather than just landing square on his own two feet forcing all of that pressure on his legs. I had the awareness to remind myself to try that. All of those thoughts coming within the two or so seconds from jump to impact. Once I hit the grass, it felt like I just kept falling and falling. I really thought I was doing the smart thing here. Maybe I was. Had I ridden the deer stand down, my placement in the stand would have put me landing on the wall that actually landed on a portion of the brush hog. Not to mention the recliner and tire rim would have landed on top of me. I would have landed on my side, back, or head. All I can do is be glad that I jumped. I have played the scenario over and over again. Wondering which would have been the best option…ride it down or jump. I'm still not completely sure. The fact still remains that I jumped. I attempted to land at an angle and lay myself down. I know my right leg hit first, then my left and attempted to roll to my side. I'm a heavy guy, I know this. The further I fell through that grass I realized this may not be good and then I hit ground. The initial shock of the force took my breath away. I still remember like yesterday. It felt like my knees were thrust into my rib cage on up into my chin. I can remember my head feeling like someone had hit it with a baseball bat. I didn't know the condition of my legs, I was just trying to get over the initial shock of landing at that point. I know I barely had any breath. I have no idea how much time has elapsed but during this time I saw the stand fall and I tried rolling away. A piece of it had apparently landed on the brush hog itself. My uncle didn't even know it had fallen. I guess you shake around so much on those tractors that most bumps and sounds go unnoticed. I saw the stand bounce and come straight for me almost like it was rolling. I don't even know how this is possible. In a split second I looked up and saw the corner of the box of the stand itself coming directly towards my face. It would have literally center cut my eyes. I raised up my left arm and put it over my face in time to catch the blow. I cannot begin to tell you the feeling of the weight and magnitude of how this thing fell on me. It literally took every ounce of energy, breath, strength and every emotion out of my body. I'm not trying to say all of this for dramatic affect. Seriously, I was limp. I vividly remember thinking while this thing is coming down on top of me, "this is how fast it can all change, and how fast you can die…just like that." At the time my Uncle did not know it had even fallen. I can only guess less than a minute had passed by now. Probably even less than that. I had so many thoughts that it all seemed like it was forever. Laying weak under that thing and half in a stagnant mud puddle, my first instinct was to get out from under it as fast as possible and get the heck away from there. I just wanted to go. Anywhere. I could still hear the tractor and things being flung around. I was panicked. I had to get away. Lodged under the stand, I couldn't see much because my arm was still wedged between the stand and my face. I took my right arm, which was about the only limb NOT under the stand and placed my palm up on the wall and tried to muster up anything I had left in me. I could still feel the weight of the wood and I couldn't breathe. I gave it everything I had. I cannot explain, nor comprehend how I got out from under the deer stand. Little did I know at the time, I had three severely broken limbs which were all trapped underneath a solid wooden structure and with one arm, I pushed it off of me. I had no other limbs to help push myself out from under it. The position of my hand was basically having to push back across my body. I had no leverage. One minute I was under, the next I wasn't. All of this happening within a few seconds. Once out from under it I was still struggling for breath and energy. I was really weak and thought I was going to pass out. At this point I leaned up to try to stand and I noticed my right leg, which took the main force of impact. It was completely shattered. I don't want to be gory but I also want you to understand that it was bad...really bad. Due to bone breakage and puncturing I had a large open wound. I tried to move it and I honestly couldn't tell if it was still attached. I laid my head on the ground and I knew I was in trouble. Surprisingly, my first thought was "Ok God, you got me." In the midst of sheer panic and trauma, my first clear thought was, "this is exactly how God gets your attention." Immediately in my head I'm pleading with Him. So many doubts I had, doubting people, doubting if He even cares, even doubting His very existence. All in the matter of a few seconds he proved his existence just by showing me the reality of the circumstances. Immediately I was reminded of the day before where I had this instinctive feeling that something bad was going to happen. It was all making sense. I felt like I was begging for my life. Begging for another chance. Again, all of this happening within a few seconds. It's as if my thoughts slowed down, but time didn't. Reality temporarily set back in as I heard the tractor shut off and my Uncle running my direction yelling for me. I could hear my dad from outside of his truck yelling for Uncle Larry, he had heard the noise and was concerned. He knew something bad had happened. I saw my Uncle and I screamed "I need help! Really bad Uncle, it's bad." I could see the look on his face when he saw my leg. I didn't even know anything else was broken at this time. I'm not sure how, but I didn't. I'm in a momentary panic. In my head I'm trying to process how an ambulance is going to make it from El Dorado to two miles deep into the woods from a total of about fifteen miles away, through traffic, and dirt muddy roads in enough time to save me. My uncle ran to the entrance lane and screamed for my dad to call 911 and get an ambulance. I heard the truck rev up and I'm not sure why he did this other than fatherly instinct but he drove that truck through that lane ramping over tree stumps and through brush with no real outlet. That truck still bears those scars today. He made it almost to me and my Uncle stopped him and made him turn around so he wouldn't see me. In the meantime, processing this information and looking at the extent of my leg injury, I realize that I may not have the hour left that it would take for an ambulance to get there. Blood loss was becoming a serious and possible issue. These next ten minutes started a life change for me that I will never be able to explain or forget.

I laid there still half in a puddle, knowing this was God. Not that I was taking it as God being this mean, vindictive person. Much like the day before I felt like I deserved it. I thought about Meg and how much I loved her. I always say "I love you" when I leave but I completely regret not hugging her. All I wanted to do was hug her. I thought about Dax and not being with him. Not being his dad or having the opportunity to watch him grow and teach him the things my dad taught me. All of this was my fault and now here I am, at the mercy of the Lord, dying. I prayed, asking God for forgiveness. Forgiveness from running. See when we run, we can only run so far before the very act invites thoughts, ideas, and actions into our lives that push us further away from our relationship with Christ. I firmly believe God never turns His back on His children, but we can get to a point that is so far away…so far gone, that our actions are all but irrelevant in the grand plan of what we are called to do for Him. I prayed that God would give me another chance. Another chance to hold my family, hold my wife and my son. Meg was seven months pregnant at the time. I wanted to see my new son. Most of all, I wanted another chance to serve God. The reality, however, had me concerned that it may be too late.

After an overwhelming wave of panic, then extreme sadness, a supernatural flow of peace and comfort rolled in. I say supernatural because I've never felt anything like it. I couldn't feel anything. No pain, no sadness, nothing but peace. In the midst of my uncle screaming, my dad ramping over tree stumps, I actually had peace knowing I was about to go. By this point I had noticed my arm, which was as bad as my leg. It was bleeding but not to the extent of my leg's injury. There was no way I could stop anything. Due to my college education, I had a small idea how my body would react with the loss of blood and I laid down and told myself, "just lay back and in a few minutes you're going to get dizzy, probably sleepy, and then you'll be with the Lord." Again, this part I struggle sharing. You may ask "Man, after all you've shared so far?" Well, yeah. The problem is I don't quite know how to explain it…and I fully realize by mentioning it I may face scrutiny from people. Having said that, I know what I experienced, and seeing that I feel like it all happened for a reason more powerful than anything I can control, I feel like it's a must share. I noticed the tall grass had been mashed down quite a bit by the force of the chaos. Paired with the lane my uncle had partially mowed, I had a pretty good view there through to the hardwood section of the property next to us. In the midst of this unexplainable peace…you know, I even hesitate using the word "peace." I don't want it to sound cliché. Somehow what I felt was more than peace? Is that even possible? Calling it peace almost taints the feeling. But in the midst of this feeling, I glanced over through that hardwood, and somewhere in the neighborhood of about a hundred or so yards, I could see my step mother Stacey calmly waking through those hardwood trees. Now I know you're saying "Hutch, really?" Honestly, I really don't care if you believe me. I know that sounds harsh, but I know what I experienced. No one will EVER take that away from me. Regardless, I can't tell you what she was wearing. Some form of white. I didn't try to lift up and call her…I couldn't move. I just laid there in awe and watched. Why her? I have no idea. I do know that we bonded shortly before her glucose accident. I know that she had seen me struggle spiritually and tried to help, and I know that if God was going to send anyone at that time to make a difference in me, that at that moment, she was the one that needed to be there…even if only an image. At the same time, if God were calling me home, seeing her definitely gave me more peace. Y'all, I had that feeling, like I knew in that moment, I was about to go home. In my mind, for some reason, God had chosen her to come meet me or whatever happens before you die. I really felt like I was in those last moments.

You know? I need you to listen to me right here. I could stop this whole story here. Right now. I could end the book. Maybe this is what you came for. Maybe this is why you're reading. You want a glimpse of hope, that something seemingly impossible, is possible with God. But I need you to know this. Look into my eyeballs! I know you physically can't right now, but figuratively... you get it. Listen, I can honestly tell you that any doubt I ever had about the existence of God, whether he loved me, whether he cared for me, any question of death, whether it stings, and quite honestly, if God EVER stops loving His Children...they were ALL answered in those few seconds. He had my complete attention and frankly, a large piece of me didn't want to leave that moment. If we claim to believe in an all knowing, all powerful God, then we have to believe that He can do whatever He wants to do, whenever He wants to do it...no excuses. My spiritual mind was so far gone, that it would take something extraordinary to get my attention. That's what He did. "God doesn't work that way anymore, Hutch!" That's exactly what I used to tell people, too. It's a laughable statement to me now. I guess my question back to you would be, "So, when did you stop believing in God?" If you can't believe that He can do whatever He wants to do, then maybe you don't really believe? All we do is preach of God's sovereignty, yet blast our own when something happens in their lives that is similar to this situation. It's already happened to me in this case. But let me say this, if that's the way you're leaning here, then take it from me, you don't want to be lying on your back in a puddle of mud, staring at the crushed bone sticking out of your leg to realize that's how God wants to remind you that He still exists in your life, and He can still do whatever He wants to do, when He wants to do it. Just remember that. Because if you're ever in that situation, at that very moment, He'll remind you of everything you said to anyone that took away from His power, and ultimately discouraged someone else from believing. He's going to get your attention. Believe me. But, even after all of that, in my situation, He wasn't done. Surprisingly, He apparently still had a lot to show me. So now you have to keep reading.

In a split second, I heard my uncle coming and I glanced over and saw him running through blood soaked grass to be by my side. I looked back over and Stacey was gone. I remember actually looking around to see if God was sending anyone else to come and help "get" me. My dad had already made his way to meet the ambulance at the highway to lead them to where I was. They were still another estimated fifty minutes away at this point. My uncle ran over and laid down next to me and held me. He grabbed me and didn't notice my arm and it got bunched up in his shirt. Warning! Y'all, my bones were broken in the middle of my forearm. Right where the deer stand came down and hit my arm when I prevented it from hitting my face. When I pulled away from my arm being trapped in his shirt, it literally made a ninety degree angle pointing down towards the ground. I caught it with my good arm, by the wrist, and calmly pulled the broken portion up and set it back into place. No pain. It was slightly amusing because I saw the look on Uncle Larry's face. His face got pale. He looked at me with the most serious "did you really just do that?" look on his face. I know my look back at him said "man I really just did that." No words, just shock and disbelief by both of us. It was nuts. We both rearranged and I tried to get comfortable next to him. This is awkward because here I am, roughly three hundred and fifty pounds and six feet tall being comforted by a man that's about 5'7" and about a hundred and twenty-nine pounds…on a good day. I'm sure it would have been somewhat amusing to see. In the meantime, however, convinced I was going Home due to eventual blood loss, I told him I needed him to calm down for a minute because I wanted to tell him a few things to tell my family. I didn't think my dad would be back in time. I knew I wouldn't have a chance to see Meg or Dax. I thought about calling her but all I could remember was throwing my phone when I jumped so I wouldn't land on it. Turns out it was in my pocket the whole time. I wanted him to tell her how much I loved her and Dax, that I always will, and to keep Dax and the new baby grounded in scripture and teach them to grow up and be respectful men. I wanted him to tell my Dad how much I loved being his son. How much I loved my brothers and for them to keep hunting, don't let this stop them…and to my Mom, I wanted her to know I forgave her. Even though some of the hurt was still there and popped up, I lived with it, and I was doing my best to get past it. The first part of that was forgiveness. All of these thoughts flowing through my head at one time and I was afraid I didn't have enough time to get them all out. He kept saying, "no you're fine, you're gonna be ok just hang in there and the ambulance will be here in a minute."

"I don't have much time" I said.

"You've got time, you're ok they'll be here in a minute."

I looked at him and said, "Uncle seriously, my leg is bad. There are lots of veins and arteries down that thing and I need to know how bad it's bleeding." I could tell there was blood on the grass around me but I couldn't tell the extent of it.

"Uncle I need you to look at it and tell me how bad it's bleeding."

"It's not bad at all, you're gonna be just fine, just a little break no big deal."

I knew it was more than that, but that's how my family is; ultra-supportive and comforting when we need it the most.

73

Finally I said, "Uncle Larry if it's bleeding really bad, I won't make it long enough for the ambulance to get here before I lose too much blood." That clicked. The moment I said that I could see in his face that he actually agreed with me and the concern and panic were written in his expression. He got up on his knees and glanced over and immediately started taking his belt off. "Is it bad?" I asked. He leaned over and started the motion of wrapping the belt around the upper portion of my leg in order to stop the bleeding. Then he paused and said, "it's clotting... it's clotting...just a little bit under the break here...it's not bleeding, it's stopped bleeding!" I laid there confused. Thankful, but confused. I still had this overwhelming amount of peace. I had no pain. I was so calm that I almost fell asleep. It's probably a good thing that I didn't but I could have. I laid there for the next forty minutes, trying to process things, yet again. Finally, it was like God told me "Just Relax." That's what I did. I didn't know how long this feeling would be there and I was going to soak it all in. I was still a little concerned and worried. More worried about my dad coming back. I didn't want him to see it. But, the peace I had surpassed that. I was almost in a daze. I remembered during my tormented ride hearing about the basketball player from Louisville who had severely broken his leg earlier that March had played his first basketball game the night before and scored his first point since his injury. I knew my leg was very similar and I thought to myself "Hey if they fixed his then mine will be ok too." The more time went on, and the more I kept staring at my leg, I began to realize that I was still a good amount of time away from an ambulance. They will probably take me to Little Rock and that's probably an hour and a half ambulance ride. Giving the remaining time for the ambulance to get there and loading me up I figured I was still more than two hours from getting solid treatment. It became very apparent that I would lose my leg. My break was below my knee and I eyeballed the distance. I knew when Stacy had to have her leg amputated due to her illness, the doctor said if they had ten centimeters below the knee that she could have a prosthetic and walk again. I knew I had at least ten centimeters there and I thought, "Ok, dude that just happened. You thought you were dying and you haven't yet, you just jumped out of a falling deer stand and broke your leg, your left leg feels funny so it's probably messed up too, and then the thing falls on you and you broke your arm...if losing your leg below the knee is all that comes from this then Praise the Lord... you're still going to be able to walk." That, coupled with the peace that I was given, fueled my drive and confidence to get better and know I was going to be ok. It was the first time in years that I had looked at a situation, a horrible situation, and found something very positive that would come from it. It actually felt great.

A few minutes later some men from the camp had rolled up. The ambulance was close and there was a forty yard walk through brush and stubble to get me to the main road. I could see the concern on their face when they saw my injuries. I mean, these are men that I've never seen so much as cry and their faces said everything. I specifically remember our good friend Danny. We had grown up with his kids Steven and Beth, and through all of those years...I didn't even know the man cried. One of the toughest men I know. He looked down at me and through those glasses I could see big tears in his eyes. He looked dead at me and said "Buddy you're gonna be ok. We're gonna get you out of here...you hang in there!" His reaction alone confirmed the seriousness. They tried to be encouraging but you could tell they were shocked and concerned. Seeing their concern just kept reiterating how bad my injuries were but I just had to keep reminding myself that I was going to be ok.

The ambulance finally arrived and it took them about fifty minutes. They must have been told that I was a big guy because there were three EMT's present. One of them came up and talked to me and took an assessment while another asked what my level of pain was. I told her not too bad but she insisted on giving me pain medication so I took it. The EMT at my feet looked at me and said "Hey Hutch can you wiggle your toes on your right foot?" he said it in a tone that led me to believe the obvious. That being that from the looks of things he didn't see there was any way I could but he had to ask. Fearing pain I held my breath and attempted to move my toes and they actually moved to which he looked extremely shocked and said "Well I'll be danged!" Now, any other person may not have found that comforting but I actually found it a little funny. Truth be told, I was actually a little shocked myself. They wrapped my injuries with temporary splints and waited for a moment. At that point the EMT looked at me and said, "Man I don't think you're going to want to ride in that ambulance all the way to Little Rock... I'm going to call in a bird." "Bird?" I asked. "Yes a Medflight Helicopter, we're gonna fly you in." Now I'm getting a little apprehensive. All I remember is television shows of these things with baskets and ropes dangling and pulling people up a hundred or so feet. I'm thinking you know we are just forty yards from the road here. Surely they know I just jumped around ten or more feet. I'm not going to be too enthusiastic about being put in a basket and lifted a hundred feet swinging around in the breeze of propellers in hopes that they can actually squeeze me in this thing. By that time Dave had gotten there. He was initially comforting and then showed his disappointment in being too late to see my actual injuries. I tried to reassure him he didn't want to see that. He was adamant. It did lighten the mood some. The EMT realized he was from the school and apparently they had landed the helicopter on the football field before for similar cases. He asked if that was possible so Dave called the school and had them prepare for me. Needless to say I was happy to be carried out on a board and not in a basket.

I can't tell you how many people were there to help carry me on that board across the brush to the road where the ambulance was waiting. I kept feeling like they were going to drop me. They kept assuring me they wouldn't. Y'all, I've said it here a hundred times…I'm a big guy. God Bless them, Ya know? I will tell you this, there's no comparison to the feeling of loved ones, albeit in the midst of this chaos, doing everything they can to get you to safety. For someone who felt so worthless before, the realization that people actually cared was something I'll never forget. I knew deep down people cared for me…but sometimes you know the enemy tempts you to believe some pretty crazy stuff.

As they carried me I could see them struggling to walk. There was a huge ditch to cross and one moment I was talking to Bob, the next he vanished. He had fallen into the ditch. They finally made it to the road and a stretcher was waiting. They put me on the stretcher and as they began to wheel me up to the doors of the ambulance I saw my dad for the first time. His face just screamed devastation, yet somehow he tried to keep a positive front. I made eye contact with him and I remember him standing right next to that stretcher and he grabbed my hand and said "I love you buddy." I lost it. "I'm so sorry, Dad." He started crying.

"Son, why are you sorry?"

"I messed up deer season, you know we look forward to this and I've messed it up."

"You haven't messed up anything, let's just get you well. You know none of this is important right now…you just get better and we have plenty of time to hunt."

They pushed me on in and closed the door. It was like a sad moment in a movie and I remember watching the doors close with my dad standing there crying but still trying to be strong. Dad went from there back to the truck and led the ambulance out of the woods. I don't even remember what direction we went out. I think the pain medicine was starting to kick in. It was much needed at this time. The roads out of the lease are old bumpy dirt roads. That ride was a bumpy one. I felt every bump. I tried to stay calm as best as I could. By the time we made it to the school I remember there were actually a lot of people there. I was laying on my back so people would come up and I remember seeing my Mom. I was just about out of it from medication at this point. I can remember being loaded on the helicopter and the on board nurse cutting my clothes off. The door wasn't even shut so that was embarrassing. What I do remember is being crammed in there and I do believe my feet were literally right next to the pilot. When they slammed the door, it squeezed me inside and I had no room. There were two nurses and one leaned directly over my face and screamed really loud. "Cannn youuu hearrr meee!? "Well, yes Ma'am I'm right here."

"We're going to put an I.V. in you, ok?!?"

I just put a thumbs up with my good hand, Ha. So they started fluids and she informed me that they were going to give me a shot that would help calm me down. She said it may affect my memory. That it did. I remember waking up a few times during the flight. When I did, I remember I could vividly imagine the feeling of falling if that helicopter door actually opened and I came out of it. That was disturbing. That's when I first realized the actual trauma I had been through. I could imagine falling and what it would feel like to land through trees or whatever we'd been flying over. About the time that I'd get worked up about it, I'd be asleep again. She woke me up as we approached UAMS in Little Rock. She warned me there would be a lot of "poking and prodding" when they wheeled me into this room and it would be immediate. We landed on top of UAMS, again, disturbing, and I remember there were no rails or anything. Just a helicopter on top of a building and although it should have be "majestic," I guess, to see all of Little Rock from the top of that hospital, it scared me to death. Heights were not my friend anymore. They wheeled me into an elevator and down to the trauma unit. I have never in my life seen the amount of people that were in there. I felt like there were at least ten different people that came around and asked me the same questions. People were, in fact, poking and prodding. I quickly realized that if someone said "I'm sorry Mr. Preston," then you better immediately brace yourself because pain of epic proportions is about to happen somewhere on your body. I heard a bunch of "I'm sorry's." Mostly from X-Ray Technicians. In the middle of everyone trying to run tests and get information, they would come in and have to X-Ray me. Every time they'd lift a leg or arm it would be excruciating. I don't know how long this ordeal lasted. I was wide awake for it. I remember laying there thinking, "Man, if this is how this is all going to go down, this is going to be horrible." The pain and stress was not friendly. I tried to stay positive. I know how close I was to death and I was trying to find every ounce of hope that I could to just be happy no matter what. About that time I saw the room clear out and it caught me off guard. A man walked in with a long white coat on. He introduced himself as one of the head orthopedists in the hospital. His name was Dr. Garrison. He kind of smiled and said "You're in rough shape!" I agreed.

"We're going to take care of you, ok?"

"Yes sir."

"Do you have any questions for me?"

"Yes, my leg… I'm going to lose it, right? Can you save it?"

He looked down at it again and Y'all, I could see the concern in his face and then he looked at me…I've never in my life seen someone be so stone cold, yet sincere, and confident at the same time. He said, "Mr. Preston, I have no idea if I can fix your leg. I really don't know yet. But I promise you something right now, if there's anyone in this hospital that can fix you, it's me…and I'm not going to let anyone else touch you." Y'all, If I could have gotten up and performed a cartwheel, I would have. He didn't guarantee me a thing but just in his simple delivery and confidence, I had faith in him. That comforted me. Not to spoil the story, but if you're ever in the Little Rock area and in need of "fixing," you better go to UAMS and let that man fix you. To this day, I won't let anyone else touch my bones, and neither will he, Ha!

From there we went and did a multitude of CT scans and then off to surgery number one. From this point, things get a little fuzzy. I remember certain events, however, I couldn't tell you a specific order they may have happened in. I do know certain things may have happened earlier in my hospital stay than later, so that's how I'll try to order them as I move on.

I want to introduce a couple of people to you. This will happen periodically as I go. Again, there are many friends and family members that came to help and visit, I wish I could acknowledge them all.

In my third year of college things were finally getting into the part of my degree plan where you had classes with other people in your degree field. The majority of your pre-requisite classes were complete and at the big university I was at, those were the classes with hundreds of people in them. As you moved later towards your field of study, classes dwindled down to very small numbers. Most of my classes for the rest of my college career ranged anywhere from twenty to twenty-five total students and that made things a lot easier because it was like high school all over again. Because they were around the same time line as you were in your degree plan, you could pretty much count on all of you being in the same classes for the rest of your career. That made it fun.

One of these classes was a teaching course, where we learned to write lesson plans for elementary physical education classes. In this particular class, we had one session a week in an actual classroom at the university, then the other days of the week we'd be at a local elementary school. Out of the twenty-five or so in the class, for each visit at a school, one of us would come up on a rotation and have to teach a specific lesson geared to a specific skill. You would have to write a lesson plan and make twenty-six copies of it. You would then line the copies out for your classmates, give one to your professor, then teach the lesson to the school children while your classmates watched you do it. It was nerve wrecking to say the least. Here's where I went wrong…

Having class at an elementary school off campus was quite stressful for me. Parking at the university was crazy and I couldn't afford to park close to my dormitory. Not to mention I usually had another class only an hour or so after the end of the off campus class. I'm not making excuses, Ha! But! I had an on campus job during the day between classes, then an evening job as well. Most of the time I wouldn't even get back to my dorm room until 10:30 at night and any homework and studying to do had to be done then. So it was easy for me to overlook things. That being said, for these off campus classes, I had to walk from my dorm room, down three flights of stairs, a few hundred yards down a hill, hopefully not in the ice, and then about a quarter of a mile to my truck. THEN drive to this school and hope I make it in time while finding a decent parking spot there too.

The first day of this off campus class I wasn't in the

rotation to teach. For some reason, I had completely misunderstood the class instructions. I had also never had this teacher and had no clue as to her personality, demeanor, or any of the sort. To explain things, the idea of the class was to get your feet wet by teaching elementary students for the first time. It also taught you how to properly write a lesson plan. In the process, the class structure was broken down into units that progressed with skills as the students learned them through the year. For example, the first lessons were on personal space. Yes, we had to teach five year old students about personal space...pure joy! After that monster was tackled we then moved to skills like running, then jumping, and progressed as the year went on. The neat part about this was everyone had a three inch thick, three ring binder and when someone gave out their lesson plan, you put that plan in your portfolio and by the end of the year, you had a folder full of lesson plans tailored to each skill to choose from and could use it for years to come. They came in handy! What I didn't understand, is that for each skill, we ALL had to write a lesson plan and bring the twenty-six copies for everyone...whether we were teaching that day in the rotation or not. Yeah. I was that guy. So I walked into class unbeknownst to the chewing I was about to withstand. I walked in and sat down by a guy named Vaden. Now I had barely met Vaden in a class before but he was the only one I kind of recognized from, well, anywhere so I decided to sit by him. Vaden was in the ROTC and on this day, I remember him being in his service blues. I'm sitting next to him with my binder and waiting to watch a fellow classmate teach away when I started noticing everyone passing out their lesson plans. Vaden looks at me, with sincere concern, and says "Hey buddy, did you not bring your lesson plans?" I kind of shrugged it off. I was nervous, but again, it was an honest mistake and I'm sure the teacher would understand. So I explained to Vaden that I didn't have them and I didn't realize we were supposed to bring them even if we weren't teaching. A crucial detail that would almost lead to an early death for me. Vaden, again, looks at me and says, "Buddy, this lady doesn't play around. If you don't have them, I don't think she's noticed you here yet, you may be better off walking right back out that door and telling her you were sick and couldn't make class today." I considered it. I really did. But I looked at him and said, "Dude, I really think it will be ok, I'll just go let her know what happened, you know, man up." He looked at me like I was dressed in white with a red sash around my neck, about to blindly run in front of a pack of raging bulls and said "I mean, if that's what you want to do, I support you" and gave me a friendly pat on the shoulder. This lady was barely five feet tall. She looked sweet. I figured I could just go up and charm her a little, tell her that I casually forgot my lessons and that I'd gladly have them there next time. She's standing alone in the middle of this gym floor, watching everyone pass their lesson plans out. I should have known this wouldn't end well. I made it about five steps off that bench towards her and it was like an owl spotted a mouse running blindly through a field and she honed in on me. She knew, Y'all. Before I even made it to her...she knew. How? Voodoo? It was like I was floating to this little woman, with her collared shirt tucked in to her wind suit pants, she stared through me the whole way. After about what seemed like a three day walk, I made it to her. I looked down at her face. She was not scared of my stature...one bit. Her words? "You didn't?"

"I didn't what, Ma'am?"

"Tell me you didn't forget your lesson plans."

"I'm sorry. I…"

"There's no sorry… you're not sorry."

What in the world!? Y'all, this lady made an example of me in front of all those people right there. About half way through the belittling, and as children were starting to make their way in, which made it worse, I looked around to check to see if my rear end was still intact. Kids were now sitting on the floor and I glared over and made eye contact with the school's P.E. teacher and as if he's seen this before, he kind of nods at me with a little grin on his face. My look back to him? "Help me," I muttered. I was on my own. My classmates were just as shocked as the children…well all of them but Vaden, who sat over with his arms crossed and his head down. It was so bad that when she was done, I asked if I could leave. Mistake number two… I was, in fact, NOT leaving. I would have to sit there and take it all in. For the rest of the hour, classmates stayed away from me like I had a bad case of the flu and a worse case of leprosy. The little kids kept looking over at me like "There's that man, the one that got in big trouble." The whole experience led to a humbling realization that if I were going to be something, I couldn't do it half way. After class I was asked to stay. She calmly told me that she didn't think she'd ever have to worry about me forgetting a lesson plan again, and she hugged my neck. She agreed from then on to walk me through any lessons that I was having trouble with, and proof any homework for any class that I had from that day forward. From that point on I had a lot of respect for her and still do to this day. She was a very integral part of me obtaining my degree and that was the only assignment I'd miss in the many classes of mine that she taught in my remaining college career. I never had lower than an A in any of her classes. She is still my friend today.

On the way out of the gym I thought I was alone. Waiting for me outside the door was Vaden. He wanted to grin but I had to grin first before he'd let go...and that's how I met Vaden. Vaden is a smart guy. He's dry humored which mixes well with my own. We did a lot of class assignments together. He invited me to his dorm room to work on a project shortly after this incident. So I made my way over. Down the hall I could hear commotion. I made the corner and saw a couple of guys standing outside Vaden's door, holding a bed mattress that had been deeply battered. One of them went flying through that mattress. Vaden held it up, and he said, "Hey Buddy, you wanna have a go?" Peer pressure got the best of me. They were all military guys so I nervously mumbled an on the spot, seemingly made up word...

"Confirmative."

I don't know...it sounded appropriate for the audience and I wanted to fit in, Ha! Then I casually put all of my two hundred plus pounds through that tiny mattress and landed safely on the floor, sliding three to four feet. Stuffing flew out the sides and upon further review, it was pronounced dead at the scene. Later in life, Vaden told me that it was that moment alone where he said "You know this guy's alright!"

We remained friends through college and there were no cell phones back then. At least I couldn't afford one. It was a lot harder to keep in touch with people than it is now. Meg and I got married and moved in to an apartment in Fayetteville while she finished her Master's Degree. I had to start a new job and the transition from college to "real life" was starting to show its strain on my anxiety. I had lost touch with Vaden for a short while until I ran into him around town. We caught up and talked about getting together for dinner with he and his wife Kathleen. Turns out, they actually lived in the apartment complex right next door to us. We were less than a hundred feet from their apartment. It was a huge weight lifted off of me. I enjoyed the new married life, but we didn't really know anyone…and having friends close really helped us adjust. Vaden could somehow sense my anxiety. Within a few seconds of being around me at any given time, if I was having a rough moment like a panic attack might be coming on, he could tell. I don't know how, I feel like I could hide them well…but he'd stare at me and say, "Come on, let's go ride around…we're getting your mind off of that." It worked. I don't think he'll ever understand how many times he actually saved me.

In that same third year, I was still in the band in college. We had a freshman join our section and at first glance, he was a little outgoing. We weren't really sure what to make of him, honestly. But he did periodically show signs of coolness so one evening we figured we'd give him a chance.

We needed to play a prank on a few girls so we staked out their location and planned to politely place things on their cars that were in good taste, but that would be extremely annoying to remove. That's when we recruited Craig. We sat around, neither of us wanting to really take the blame for what was about to happen, nor did we want to get caught in the act. So we conjured up a scheme to get the new guy, whom this group of girls didn't even know existed, to do our dirty work for us. To our surprise, he was all for it. He really didn't know what he was in for. So we drug him along in the back seat of a car. There were about 6 of us piled in that thing…leading him on as if we were going to park and all get out and help. We pulled up to the surprisingly well-lit house and stopped the car. We started to climb out, sending Craig out first. When he made it out, we quickly climbed back in, threw a couple of tubes of toothpaste and a can of shaving cream out the window and sped off. Looking back, it was wrong of us to do that. They didn't know him and if he were to have gotten caught, they would have definitely called the police on him. Like a trooper, as we sped away, he started hammering the pre specified cars. We made the loop, came back expecting him to jump in the car out of fear, but he smiles and waves us on for another loop. The guy wasn't scared at all. He was born for this. As we made the second loop, we knew we had stumbled upon a future legend. A diamond in the pranking rough. He was a keeper. "This guy's alright." On the fourth lap of the neighborhood, we knew his loyalty had been more than tested. We had to get him out of there. Y'all, we had to force him back into the car. That's how I met Craig.

Later in his college career Craig became one of the mascots at the university and his legend lived on. Craig's mascot days were short lived as he was accused of dropping a cardboard trash receptacle down from the upper deck of the basketball arena, in full mascot uniform…for fun. Although he denies the severity of it, upon hearing of the incident, it was no surprise to me or anyone who knew him, alas, his duties as mascot were short lived. His talent was recognized by the company that makes the air inflated costume that he donned and hired him to do their large, important corporate events. He's a natural. He currently works in sales and is quickly working his way up the corporate ladder with a pretty high end job for a large wipe manufacturer…and moonlights as inflatable cartoon characters. It's hilarious.

Craig will be the first to tell you that the only emotion he really knows how to process and project is sarcasm. He works hard, too hard sometimes, but when push comes to shove, he'll break his back to be there for his family and friends. That's why Craig is important to a lot of people.

Now, back to surgery and stuff…I do remember I was in a ton of pain. Surgery one basically repaired my arm and cleaned my right leg. I think the arm was going to be easiest to repair so they hit that first. From that point on, the arm was ok…kind of. During the surgery they had to insert two metal plates down my forearm. Due to the amount of reconstruction and plate placement, they had to make an incision on either side of my forearm. They pretty much run the length of my wrist to my elbow. There was significant tissue damage on the inside of my arm during the repair that I was given the option to either have them sow it up, or they could actually place a skin graft over the egg sized hole that was left. According to the doctor, sewing up the hole could lead to unsightly rippling of the skin because they would basically have to tie it shut and it would draw up like an old pair of gym shorts. So I took the option of having a skin graft. For the graft, they asked if I would mind an experimental procedure using what they call Integra Matrix. Keep in mind, I'm semi-conscious on some ridiculously awesome pain medication during these questions. From what I was told, Integra Matrix is a cross linked bovine tendon collagen. That's right, I said "Bovine," as in "cow," and a silicone substance that together is porous. Now I'm explaining this NOT as a medical professional, but instead, how I interpreted the explanation and how all of this was going to work. As I would learn later with my "bad" leg, skin grafts are very fragile. So this process would allow for tissue to grow without the repeated layering and layering of my own tissue to form a base. After this concoction set up for a while, they would then only need a very thin layer of my own tissue to cover the wound and it would attach and begin to grow like normal. So that's what we did with the arm.

After surgery one I remember waking up in the recovery area. I didn't really know where I was. I have had surgeries before so I figured I was in recovery but I was pretty much out of it. I just remember being really thirsty and I was in a lot of pain. I begged for something to drink and I specifically asked for Sprite which they gave me. Any of you who have had surgery before knows that when they put you to sleep, it feels like you just immediately wake right back up and that's what it did for me, but somehow I knew I had been out for some time. I didn't know for how long, but it was a while. I was heavily sedated but I remember being wheeled up and when I made it into my room, the first two people I remember seeing was Vaden and Craig. I was coherent enough to look at a nurse with a straight face and tell her that I didn't want that guy (Vaden) in my room. Later, I had to convince her that it was a just a joke. Details really got fuzzy here. That's about all I remember of that moment and I'm pretty sure I passed smooth out. Later that evening, at some point in the middle of the night, I woke up and looked over towards the window. I could make out the rear end of a male figure laying down on a couch that was in the room. In my sedated state, I was trying to figure out who in the world it was. Early in my hospital stay they would come in and take vitals and draw blood. In that process they would turn a small light on. When they did, I noticed it was Vaden laid over there facing away from me, curled up on that hard lumpy couch that was about a foot too short for his body. No blanket. No pillow. Y'all…I cried. I had experienced so much already, and truthfully, had felt worthless up until the accident…but that someone who I knew was a friend, but actually cared enough about me to make sure I wasn't going to be there alone. I mean. Wow… It turns out he told my family to go get some rest and since he was there he'd stay with me. Then Craig stayed the next night. They had driven down together when they heard the news of the accident. I can't begin to tell you how much they mean to me. I have a number of close friends and many of them were involved in this whole ordeal. I'll mention more of them as I go, but I wouldn't have made it through without any of them.   I was able to see through this foggy lens that people actually cared. People were willing to help me, and God was beginning to do something special. I just had to take a moment and let it all happen. Stop fighting things, and let it all go. This whole journey, as you will see, will have many ups and downs. There are times as I've already mentioned where I felt next to God Himself. Then there are times where I would almost hit rock bottom. In the end, these circumstances, with the help of God, family, and great friends, will help change my life forever.

# 6

# F-921

One of the first things I remember from lying the in hospital is a friend of mine coming to see me. I was barely coherent from all of the sedation but I know it was the first time I had seen him cry. He had just lost a friend in a hunting accident similar to mine, but he didn't make it. It was emotional for him and rightfully so. He didn't stay long, but he prayed with me and went on his way. There were a lot of things that started happening that showed me how big of a deal this was. I knew I was in bad shape, but like I said before, I didn't think too much of myself and I was really surprised people actually cared. Another friend of mine from Northwest Arkansas burst into the door and was extremely relieved. All he had heard was that I was on a life flight to Little Rock and it wasn't good. He honestly thought I wasn't going to make it. I had heard rumors that I had died. With social media rampant in today's society, word gets around fast and everyone wants to be a part so badly, that information is shared and sometimes it just gets miscommunicated. But, the more attention that was brought to my incident, I started to fully take in how serious the whole ordeal was. I already knew how fast I could die. How quickly it could end. But, even in that, I guess it was some weird coping mechanism, but I had convinced myself that my injuries were bad, but on the minor side of bad… if that's even a thing. I really thought they'd be repaired fairly quickly and although it would take time to heal, it'd be a piece of cake…so I thought.

I had many, many visitors. You would think someone in my situation would rather not have them…but they kept me going. I loved seeing people and talking. That's odd because my mindset before the accident was completely opposite. But, it brightened my day to see people come in. Someone brought me a neck pillow. I still have that thing. It was wonderful! I had about a dozen cases of sprite in the room. People knew I liked sprite, so they would just bring it by the case. I had a friend and when we were in high school she had a car wreck. I went to see her in the hospital and we had a baseball game later that evening. She said, "If you play, hit me a homerun!" I didn't play much that season, but miraculously I got in the game, and hit my only home run that season. I took her the homerun baseball when the game was over. After fourteen years, she still had that baseball. She brought it to me and said, "Well it helped me get better then, maybe it will help you now!" That was a special moment. The outpouring of love from everyone really touched my heart. I truly think it helped in my recovery.

There were many positive moments, but they were all had while fighting through massive amounts of pain. If my hospital stay had a last name, it would be "pain." I don't recall the order of many of my surgeries. As I said, most of the time I was so sedated, that I remember things, but they were in spurts and I'm not sure exactly when they happened, only that they happened. I fell in a mud hole. It was full of dirty, muddy water. In the process of trying to escape from the fallen stand, somehow I just kind of got it all in my open wound. Infection was the biggest concern for that leg and the possibility of keeping it. Every time I would go to surgery for something, even if it was to repair that arm, they would "pressure wash" that leg. That's the term they used. I'm not interested in the process. I believe them!

My left ankle was severely damaged. A few years prior, I had been cleaning an elevated flower bed for my mother-in law and as I was stepping off the bed, I came down on a tree root and suffered a severe sprain. For years I had issues with that ankle. I had already developed severe arthritis in the joint. I had it x-rayed then and the doctor said there may have been a hair line fracture but there wasn't much they could do about it. This accident didn't help matters. I had broken the bottom portion of the tibia bone that connects with my foot to form the ankle joint. Not only was it broken and separated from everything, every ligament in that joint was either torn, or stretched so badly that it was almost irreparable. After they fixed my arm, and while they were taking time to make sure infection didn't set in on my right leg, they went in to start repairing and salvaging my ankle. Every time the orthopedist would work on it, he would come back and talk about all the arthritis he was dealing with and he was puzzled at the amount of it. I wasn't thinking straight enough to explain that past injury, but once I did, it made a lot of sense to him. But he would always "warn" me about the amount of arthritis I was going to have to deal with in that joint for the remainder of my life. He wasn't lying. To this day, other than scarring, the only painful reminder and source of any limping that I have isn't from my bad leg, but from that ankle joint. There are days where I can't even stand to walk on it. But, in the process of repairing, he had to insert a metal plate with screws and fasten that all back together. He also drilled and inserted pins to help re-route my tendons and ligaments to see if they would tighten back up and heal. Once that was accomplished, that ankle stayed in a cast for weeks to just let things heal. I remember the hours after that surgery. I don't know what they did in there, but for over twenty-four hours, I didn't open my eyes much, but in my sedation, I remember it feeling like my whole left leg and foot were twisting around. I could close my eyes and it felt like someone was literally standing at the foot of my bed twisting that thing… pain and all. Whatever they had to do to it had to have been really traumatic for those nerves. They were going crazy.

The worst injury I had, as I've mentioned, was my right leg. It took the brunt of my fall. I had a compound fracture of my tibia and fibula. Those are the two main leg bones below the knee. Not only were they fractured, but crushed as well… there were pieces of them throughout my leg. As a matter of fact, checkup x-rays taken a year after the accident still showed small bone fragments in my leg. There was so much going on with this injury. Not only were they fighting infection constantly, they were also going to have to literally piece the bones back together like a puzzle and somehow get them strong enough to bear weight again. Everyone knew it was going to be a challenge. My dad would come up for every surgery. I remember him talking about the doctor working on me for hours and then coming in to the surgery waiting area to update my family and saying, "We're making progress, but I'm tired. I really need to get some rest and let him also rest for a day or so. Then we'll get back to it." Later, they finally got my leg in good enough shape to put the nail through it. Now, what they referred to as a "nail" was actually a titanium metal rod that would be threaded through my tibia, the bigger bone, then fastened in to give both the bone and the leg strength while it healed, and after healing. In the doctor's own words, "We need to get this tibia healed, we're really not concerned with the fibula right now." The Fibula being the smaller, skinnier leg bone. He told me that it didn't bear much weight and if we had the strength of the rod, then it wouldn't matter. I trusted him. The process of inserting the nail is pretty much as self-explanatory as it sounds. The doctor cuts a small incision in the knee, cuts through the patella tendon to expose the top of the tibia, drills a hole through to the center of the tibia, inserts a guide wire for the nail itself, then literally hammers the nail down the guide wire, through the leg and bone fragments, then screws the nail in place. The bone will eventually heal around the nail and screws, giving some pretty solid support. I bet you're thinking, "Wow, that sounds painful!" You're exactly right. It was very painful. When the nail was inserted, it was a huge step for my leg…pardon that pun, but we weren't out of the woods yet. Boy, puns all around.

When the nail was finally inserted, I remember my dad telling me he spoke with the doctor about how things were going. Dad is always worried about us and through our life, it seems if there is any negative information that may be coming our way, I think he'd rather be the one to share it with us. He's protective. He can relate that information and be the rock there for us when we need it. I'm so thankful for that. I know Dad was concerned about me eventually losing my leg. He wanted to be prepared for that and if there was a real chance, he wanted to know first. He didn't want a doctor coming in and sharing that news. I think a lot of it is he wanted to also know for himself. Obviously he was worried, but if he could get over the shock and sadness first, then maybe he could be in better spirits and better equipped to be there for me in the event that we had an amputation ahead of us. He pulled the doctor to the side in the waiting area and just simply asked, "Is Hutch going to lose his leg? I need to know what you're really thinking."

"Mr. Preston, I really don't have an answer for that yet. It's just too early to tell. We're expecting circulation issues, but if he has good blood flow, we may be ok. Does he drink alcohol? Does he smoke? Do any drugs?"

"No, he's never had alcohol. He's never smoked. He doesn't do any drugs. He's a big buy and likes food… those are the only health related issues he has."

"Well, if you're right, and he hasn't done any of that stuff, he'll have clean blood, and we should be able to save it with no problems. My main concern was having enough clean blood to have the proper circulation to heal it all up."

"That's wonderful news."

You can take that for what it's worth. I'm not going to sit and debate drug, alcohol, and smoking issues. Whether you're addicted or just recreational, that's something you have to deal with and decide whether it's right for you and your family. I'm in no place to point fingers. But I know one of the major factors in still having my own leg attached to my body is because I've chosen to stay away from those three things. I'm not implying that you're going to lose your leg tomorrow if you happen to find yourself in the same situation, but for my situation, this is what helped me. I know I struggle with many other things, but would strongly recommend doing what you can to eliminate one or all of these things from your life. As crazy as it may sound to you, that one recreational choice could lead to a lifetime of addiction, and that addiction could one day leave you without a limb if you were ever in a situation that is similar to mine… not to mention many other problems in your life.

During this healing process, I have to commend the hospital staff. They answered to my every whiney, mostly incoherent need. Every time one of them would come in, it was like I asked for an additional pillow. My bed was full of pillows. It was a process. I wanted everything elevated. True story here. I had three pillows elevating each of my legs, and one stuffed between them so they wouldn't migrate and roll down to the center of the bed and cause me more pain. I had two under each arm so I could just lay them there and relax. One under my head sitting below that fancy neck pillow and one more just in the event that I lost one. I don't know what caused me to itch so much, but I did so constantly. I requested a back scratcher and I believe Meg brought me one. Another friend had overheard me asking for one, so they brought me another back scratcher and it just happened to be the same kind as the other one! This was great. I had a "sterile" one and "non-sterile," you know, depending on where the itch was.

I would barely eat. Most of the stuff I didn't want to eat anyway. I'd try to get protein, but I didn't like the way I had to go to the bathroom. It was miserable. So, I didn't eat much.

Now, I don't know how much protein is actually in a hospital hamburger patty, but that's about all I would eat for a week or two. I remember the nutrient nurse would come in and bring me a cheeseburger. I had options, don't think I didn't. I just always chose the cheeseburger. It reminded me of the one they had in the cafeteria in elementary school. I didn't want the bun, so I remember Cliff peeling the bun off, leaving cheese only, cutting the patty up and feeding it to me so I wouldn't have to move. Later my nutritional nurse talked me into a taco salad. UAMS has a wonderful taco salad. By the end of my stay, we had about three items we rotated around. It got to the point where I just told her to surprise me. There were times where she'd come in to take my order and say, "I'm gonna bring you a cheeseburger. You don't want what they have down there today." I was thankful. My main objective was to just lay there, rest, and heal. I had to do whatever it took to keep progressing. Even if it was eating even the slightest of bits

Amongst that mountain of pillows was my left arm. With my left arm in the process of healing, I was paranoid that something would happen to it. To this day I don't have full range of motion in it and although I haven't confirmed it yet, I am afraid that's because I didn't really rehab it as well as I should have while in the hospital. They would send therapists to work on it, but all I was being told by plastics was to be careful for the graft because it's fragile. Not to mention I had stitches on the back side of that arm from my elbow to my wrist. On the front side, I had about five inches from elbow down, then an egg-shaped hole, then another three to four inches of stitches to my wrist. I was fitted one day for a custom stabilizing cast that held it in a bent "L" shape. So, as timid as I was about it, someone coming in and telling me that I needed to remove the contraption that was keeping it stable, so that she could move the arm around freely, didn't make much sense to me. Looking back on things, I should have asked more questions. Maybe I'd have my range back. But all I knew at the time was that it was to remain still. On top of all of that, to make matters worse, I sure wasn't letting someone stick a needle in it for any reason at all. That left my right arm to be the I.V. and blood drawing arm. That got old really quick. Eventually, there weren't many places to stick anymore. I was given the option to have a PICC line inserted. That stands for Peripherally Inserted Central Catheter. I know, it's a mouthful. They basically put a port in your arm and run a thin line through a vein to your heart. It's basically for long term I.V. situations and drawing blood. I was a little nervous at first, but if it kept me from being poked every four hours, I was willing to give it a go.

So, they had to perform the procedure in a sterile environment. I figured I'd be wheeled to another surgery but no, they cleared out ole F-921 and a gentleman walked in and preceded to start cleaning the room. He wasn't a bundle of personality. His bedside manner was lacking. But at the time, I figured, "You know, if I was having to insert this line, I'm the doctor, and I'm having to sterilize a room for my own procedure, I'd be pretty aggravated too." So, I gave him the benefit of doubt. He was in some form of white coat I think I remember. He had a mask on, so I just assumed doctor. What did I know? About that time a little girl walked in. I'm not kidding. She couldn't have been a day over thirteen. It's an event that still puzzles me to this day. So, she walks in and starts looking around. I watch her put a mask on herself. Wearing a white coat. Y'all, my exact thought… "Awe cool, they're letting this middle schooler come shadow this doctor today." You know, it's a medical school as well, why not? I hope he's good you know? Maybe she can learn something positive today? She finishes tying her mask on, starts gloving up, and grabs the ultrasound machine HE, or so I thought, was going to use to find the proper vein for the port. As she's wheeling it over to me, I hear him speak, this mid-forties aged man addresses this mid-thirteen aged girl, with some of the most terrifying words I had heard spoken to that day in that very hospital... "Excuse me Doctor, would you like me to lay out some extra gauze?" Y'all, in the middle of taking a sip of MiraLAX laced apple juice, I shot a ten-foot stream of it across the room, spewing from my mouth and said "Doctor?!?" I'm reaching around. Grabbing my trapeze bar above my head with my good arm. Looking for the nurse call button with my bad arm. I'm trying to run away on both of my bad legs while continuously screaming "No she is not! She is absolutely not!" Y'all, I'm scared to death. I look over at her, now standing within arm's length, I know this because, well, she had my arm in her hands scanning it for a vein. I'm thinking this girl was just playing with an easy bake oven yesterday, now she's about to stick a five-foot string of fishing line through a hole she's about to make in my arm...no way. Then she looks up at me, pulls the mask down, and square in the eyes, Y'all (I can't make this up), with this RUSSIAN accent, says "You big baby, calm down...stop being big baby." I'm like, "Where did THAT (pointing at her mouth) come from?!" Y'all I'm sweating! "You don't have a driver's permit! Who are you calling baby!" She was not amused. Neither was her partner, in whom I now have figured out his aggression is probably coming from having to work for a thirteen and a half year old Russian doctor. The last thing I remember is asking her if it would hurt. She laughed at me. Strike two. She then informs me there are no nerve endings in my veins and I won't feel a thing. So, I laid there. Accepting whatever fate she may bring me. My life, seemingly in the hands of a child, behind a mask. But, she was right. I didn't feel anything. Probably because I was passed out from the trauma of being the subject of a weird Russian medical experiment. Who knows? In the end, I gave her a stuffed animal for all of her hard work. Seriously though, all kidding aside, she did a great job. When I knew I was going to survive, I told her she did great and I appreciated her work. She smiled, did a cartwheel, and went on out the door. Ok, I made that part up, but still, the PICC line made a huge difference. I was able to get rest during the night. They could draw blood and I wouldn't even wake up. Being put to sleep for surgeries was also easier and less stressful. It was a great choice all the way around.

The nursing staff was nothing short of amazing. If I try to name them all, I would forget someone and I'm not even going to try. I had a great nurse on day one. She was there for two or three days and then went out of town on vacation. I remember being really disappointed, but every single one after her was just as great! Guys would sit down and talk sports with me after giving me doses of medicine. Others would share edible arrangement gifts from visitors because I couldn't eat them all. Some would sing, and one sweet lady helped keep my wounds clean, and washed my hair every day! I had faith knowing they would be there for me as soon as I pushed my little button. They made my stay easy and I'm so grateful.

As always, when entering a facility for healthcare, you have to list your daily medications and doses. I was on a certain type of medication to keep a portion of my anxiety at bay. It wasn't the nursing staffs fault. No one really explained it to me. I just know when they would come in, they would call that medication something completely different. It puzzled me, but I wasn't too concerned. There was a resident doctor that would come in every morning and assess me. I just randomly asked her why that medication didn't have the same name as the one I had been taking, you know, for the last five years. She told me although they had different names, they were the same medication. Now, I didn't realize this was a huge issue until I got home a few months later and had a checkup with my primary care physician…that's when he broke the news to me. They were not the same medications. They were actually two different kinds. Now, there could have been a medical reason as to why the previous wouldn't work and/or wasn't safe for me to take during this time. If that's the case, no one told me. Yes, they both treated the same issues, but the previous was a long term medication. It stuck with you for a while…like twenty-four hours. The other was fast acting but wasn't extended release. I should have been taking it at least 2 times daily. At least that's how it was explained to me. Regardless, it's not healthy to abruptly stop taking these medications, especially if you've been taking them for a while. I had abruptly stopped. Which means after a week or two, it was completely out of my system…and the new medication could take four to six weeks to get set in my system. Now, everything I will explain to you in the next few chapters may make a little sense!

I started feeling the effects of not having that medication around week three of my stay in the hospital. It started to get pretty brutal. It didn't help that this was the time where Mom had to go back to work, Meg was trying hard to rest, and I was having to adjust to staying more nights at the hospital alone. I guess some of you may think that's not that big of an issue, but put yourself in that situation one day, and it will be. If it wasn't for me being friends with all of the nursing staff, it would have been even worse. But, I could feel my anxiety starting to take over my stay there. Panic was setting in here and there and it became really hard to fight the attacks off. I didn't understand why. I just attributed it to being tired and just a byproduct of being in the hospital for weeks. It's totally plausible. As you will find out, it lasted for a long time during this process while those medications were out of whack. This caused me to start slipping back into the cracks that I was in before the accident. I knew it would be a roller coaster, but this was the start of it. I think I did well at hiding it most of the days. I got emotional a lot. But I remember starting to feel sorry for myself, and that's just something you can't let happen. I was cheery with the majority of the staff, but inside I was really dealing with some things. During my stay there, there was a bad ice storm that left most of the staff stranded at the hospital. I remember having the same nurse for five straight days. Mom had come up and got stuck in the weather as well. But, this nurse couldn't go home, so she just stayed on and worked. When you're practically stranded for that long, sometimes people open up when they wouldn't any other time. During that time she came in and I was a little emotional. She made sure I was ok and we talked about a few things and I just excused it off as being tired of lying there every day…it was starting to wear on me but I'd be ok. She came back hours later with a sign she had colored with markers. It was just a simple sheet of notebook paper that had the colorful words, "BELIEVE," written really big and then a small, "You've got this!" below. She went and stuck it on the wall in front of my bed and she said, "Now if you ever feel that way again, just read that!" It made me feel better. I had new encouragement! A bit later she came back in. I was feeling a lot better and told her I appreciated it. I knew we had talked about her Faith at one point, and I asked her if there was anything I could pray for her about. She shared with me that her mom had just had a bad medical diagnosis that could potentially be deadly at any moment. She went on to tell me that she was worried, but had faith it was going to be ok. She would leave work, when not stranded, and go take care of her mother when she was done at the hospital. Her story made me tear up and start crying again. Crying was becoming a pretty common thing for me. But she said, "No, don't cry, it's ok…I don't want you getting upset about it."

"But I am. It's not your fault, and I'm going to pray with you about it. But, I'm more upset with myself. I mean, how selfish of me to assume that I'm the only one around here going through difficult times. Here I am laying out all of my worries and stresses, and you have some of your own that you're dealing with."

You know I learned a lot that night. I knew I wasn't the only one with problems. This woman had been stuck in the hospital for days, probably worried sick about her mother, and I was just pity partying away right in front of her like I couldn't care less about anyone else's problems! From then on I tried to start being thankful for my situation. It could have been a lot worse. I realize that. That didn't mean the enemy wasn't going to keep fighting me. Like I said, emotionally, I'd go up and down, but I had to keep fighting. I wanted to make sure that I looked after and cared for other people's feelings as well. God could use my situation as a support system to help other people through their tough times. Throughout this whole recovery time, people would come up to me and say, "I thought I was going through some stuff, but then I look at you and I think I'm not going through nothing like you are." You know, I had felt that way before. I'd reply back, "Maybe, but pray hard and I'll pray for you. Because you don't know how this feels until you've been through it. Neither do I know what it feels like to go through what you're going through. But, don't ever discount your struggles based on someone else's. If you feel pain, physical or emotional, it's real to YOU! Pray about it, and don't ever be ashamed or afraid to ask someone for prayer…no matter how small you think your problems are. They're big to you… and you deserve the same prayers and strength from God to make it through." So, I guess what I learned here is I'm not the only one hurting. At the same time, I can't brush my feelings of pain and hurt under the rug just because someone's problems seem worse than mine. Every one of us has issues that we deal with daily. The moment we start comparing our problems and worries with other people's problems and worries, it leaves us in a state of doubt and confusion, which ultimately leads us to more pain.


Shortly after Meg and I got married, we found a church that we both came to enjoy. We had some friends attend there and they invited us to come. We developed some great relationships there. Year after year we were able to ease in and feel like we could serve again. I had always felt a call to ministry, but didn't really know how to get to that point or where to start. Eventually a staff change lead the church to seek out a new youth minister. I had spent time with some friends leading worship for the youth program there with the previous youth pastor. When he was called elsewhere, we were asked if we would fill in until one was found. I happened to take the role of giving messages on Wednesday nights. I loved it. I felt like I was finally able to be a part of what God was doing in a church and answer a call that I felt like I had. For a few months I was able to bond with those kids. I wasn't sure if it was helping them at the time, but it was doing wonders for me. Numbers were rising in the program. We seemed to have a good thing going. I talked to Meg one evening and we both started praying about how we should pursue a future in ministry. After a short time I put my name in for the position at that church. After interviewing and going through the long process, I was told that I didn't have the necessary credentials to fully execute the job. Now this may sound like I'm angry, I'm not…but it hurt…really bad. I felt like everything I had just done, time that was put in, prayer, money I had spent on things…was for nothing. I felt used. I started comparing my "credentials" to my dad's and it hurt more because I knew the things he had accomplished for the Lord…and his credentials were pretty much the same as mine at the time. So was all of the work God did through him not good enough? Would I never be able to serve? Y'all, it was very hard to get over. It wasn't as much anger as me feeling inadequate. Not to mention I had put my trust in another church, and it seemed to let me down again. I truly felt like I put my heart and soul into that program and those kid's lives. We had some great times in those few months. But the feeling I had now made me embarrassed. It made me feel like I didn't do a good enough job, and if one of those kids stumbled, it was my fault because I wasn't good enough. I put a lot of pressure on myself.

Shortly after that, the church hired another man. I did what I could to help him transition into the program. I did my best to hide my feelings from him to keep the program moving forward. Some of the kids were angry so I tried to stay out of the way a bit to let him get adjusted and smooth things out. Wes ended up being a great friend and still is today. Honestly I don't even know if he knows what happened...I don't think I ever opened up to him about it because I didn't see it as being appropriate. If God decided to put him there, then I couldn't get in the way. In the months and years after, I couldn't let that hurt go. It wasn't necessarily this specific instance, but things within that church surfaced and when you put all of that on top of what I had experienced and was struggling with from my past, it was pretty much that straw the enemy used to kick me down for a very long time. I wanted to be near God...but I didn't want to be near a church. I kept a bunch of that stuff hidden inside. It festered. I showed an outward "joy" but it wasn't there. I tried to act like I was supposed to, but I was in a deep dark pit and it was getting worse. I have huge regrets and I often wonder what I missed and how God could have used me if I would have stopped acting like a baby, picked myself up and got back on the ole horse. But I didn't. Wes ended up leaving that church to go pastor his own. He needed a youth pastor and shortly before my accident he gave me a call. I was truly honored. I went in to meet with him and I knew my heart wasn't in the right spot. I had no business, with my mindset at the time, being in that situation and I told him that I was struggling with some things within my heart. He told me to take some time and pray about it. I knew God could fix it...but it was bad. I had a ton of anger. Sadness. Guilt. Shame. I mean, I could go on. But the enemy had me pinned down so bad. This was a few months before my accident. I left Wes' office that day and told him I would pray about it and let him know. Like a big fat jerk, I never came back… and it's one of the biggest regrets that I've ever had. I am so sorry. I let the enemy wrap me up so hard that I completely neglected a friend, mentor, and whoever God would have used me to help, save, change… I know I've told him how sorry I am, but I don't know if he will ever truly understand the guilt I have over that. He's still my friend to this day. Every time he sees me, he prays with me, no matter where we are. It means the world to me. I will forever be grateful for his friendship.

So while I was leading those young people, I spoke about issues and things that I felt called to speak on. Sometimes it got a little uncomfortable and that's kind of what I wanted. Sometimes as young people (and adults) we put ourselves in situations that we should never be in. I wanted to let them know they were leaders. They were role models. There was a young lady that would come sit in the back. She was a junior or senior at the time and a regular attender with her family. From what I could tell she was fairly popular at her high school. I'd get about half way into the message and she'd just get up and storm off. At first I passed it off as nothing. Then week after week she kept doing it. When things got a little awkward, she bolted. I wasn't trying to attack her. Actually there were times where I didn't even really know what I said to make her leave. I tried to excuse it as maybe she had a job? But it kept happening and I thought "Man, I really don't think I'm saying anything that would be THAT offensive to her." I really didn't know what was going on but she was never around for me to attempt to talk to her and hash out some concerns…but I could tell by the look on her face she was dealing with some things. So, for some reason, I just let her be. I really thought she hated me and I thought I'd let her sort out whatever she was dealing with on her own. I don't know if it was a good idea, but I didn't stop or alter what I was speaking on. I just kept going and when I'd go home, I would pray, and pray, and pray for her. I didn't even know what to pray for, I just felt like I needed to.

I shared all of that story to help you further understand my mindset when the accident happened. But also to show you how God used those situations to show me exactly what I needed so see. So, I'm lying in the hospital bed and drowsy from a surgery I had that morning. My mom is over in the recliner next to me and we are both sleeping. I heard the door open but I kept my eyes closed and thought if whoever wanted to see me felt like waking me up, they could do so. So I laid there with my eyes closed and I felt someone grab my hand. I looked up and it was her. The girl from youth group. Older now, engaged, and she seemed so happy. She was a nursing student there at the hospital and had heard about my accident. When I saw her Y'all I lost it. I didn't have to say anything, she didn't have to say anything, I just fell apart and she did too. My mom woke up and I'm sure it was awkward for her because I knew mom didn't have a clue who she was. She didn't say much, but she said "Can I pray for you?" So I let her pray for me and I know I say things like "they will never know how much it meant to me," but seriously, I had a lot of these "never know" moments during this ordeal and this was one of the most powerful. There I was, with a girl that was a student that I was convinced hated the ground I walked on. In her own way, she apologized, she was compassionate, and God used her to show me that maybe, just maybe, I was relevant in someone's life…and it was someone that I NEVER expected to be relevant in at all. On top of that, she was praying for ME! I was a mess, Y'all. The visit wasn't long, she let me get back to resting, but when she left mom looked at me and said, "I have no idea who she was but she is special." I said, "Mom, you don't know the half of it."

Later I reached out to her and was able to send her a message thanking her for being there for me. I shared with her that it was completely unexpected because I pretty much thought she hated me. But I told her I prayed for her daily during that time. When she responded she filled me in on some things she was dealing with and what's crazy is she was having some of the same struggles with people and church that I was having. She told me "You sending up some unknown prayers for me might have been the only thing that kept me from going off the deep end." She went on to say that she had grown closer to God during her college years and she was a whole new person. It was truly a blessing. I asked her if she minded if I shared this story and she was very receptive to the idea. For the sake of her privacy, I decided to not reveal her name, but I want her to know I'm so proud of what she has become and she's a huge example of what the Lord can do for, and through someone! There are a handful of those students that I still keep in contact with and I'm so proud of all of them.

Never, in a million years, would I have ever thought that God would use a student like that to show me some of the most important things during this healing and restoration time. For once I felt relevant. Most of all, God was showing me that I don't need immediate return and gratification from doing His work to feel like I'm important in His eyes. Just do the work. You never know who you're touching, or how God is using you. You don't have to be talented. You don't have to have special college degrees. Just do the work and we may never see a reward until we get to Heaven, but it's not even about a reward, Y'all. It's about fulfilling what God has put us on this Earth to do. Laying in that hospital bed, I still have a long way to go, but I'm finally starting to realize what God is doing. He's showing me things and not only am I relevant, but I'm learning how easy it is to get distracted. How easy it is for the enemy to kick us while we're down. To deceive us. To make us feel unworthy. We're not good enough. Y'all, every one of us struggles with something. It's our decision if we're going to let the enemy use that to cripple our ministries. It's easy to let him do it, and if you're not careful, you'll wind up spending a lot of time having to heal and get it back.

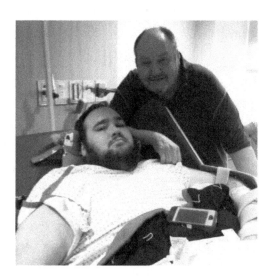

# 7

# RESTORATION

I'll be honest, I carried a lot of anger with me after Mom left our family. I wouldn't say it was the sole source of everything I had put myself through, but to say the whole situation didn't affect me long term, would be a huge understatement. I don't need to go too far into describing my emotions at the time. All of those things are irrelevant at this point in my life. It's crazy, though what the enemy can use to destroy, or attempt to destroy someone's life…even if it wasn't their decision to begin with. It was definitely a shock to my everyday life and it caused me to lose trust in a lot of people. When you let those kinds of anger form a pit in you that just keeps festering, there is a very small chance that you will come out ahead in the long run. Those simple things that you are usually able to let go of so quickly, become a nuisance and are mentally blown way out of proportion. Over time, that anger builds up in to a bitterness that has no place in your life. Ever.

I'll be the first to admit that I clung to my dad when Mom left. I had no other option. With my anxiety the way it was, I needed a source of strength and comfort. That was missing. So

I clung to whatever I had, and that happened to be Dad. This isn't discrediting my relationship with my father by any stretch. We already had a great, close relationship. But this event clearly made it stronger. I was unwillingly forced to choose a side whether I realized it or not. My dad was hurt. It hurt him bad. But I can't remember a time where he just openly talked bad about my mom after she left. I truly think his goal was for her to finally come home one day. He did everything he could to make sure if and when she came back, things would be back to normal. The longer things went and she didn't return, slowly hope diminished. For me, the longer she was gone, the harder it got. The harder it got, the angrier I would get. For some reason it felt like I had to be angry at her in order to let her "go." Looking back, I don't think that's the clear answer, but at that time, it worked. I want you to understand this isn't a "Mom Bashing" session. Hopefully, through my story, I can relate to someone out there and share how God allowed me to overcome some of these issues. The last thing I want is for her to read this and feel guilty and worse about the situation. It's a part of my life and a part of this story. Both she and I feel like it needs to be shared.

It took a few things happening in her own life to begin to mend the relationships. I know she tried for a lot of years. I don't know that I was as ready as my brothers. We spoke and I feel like I acted like everything was ok, and I need you to know that I didn't, under any circumstances, hate, or harbor any feelings of hatred towards her. It just hurt. I took it personal for a really long time. I tried to be happy around her and I feel like I was, but deep down I knew there was something that just ate at me. When I would come home to visit, I would stay with my dad. I always stayed with him. I'd make a point to see her on the way out of town. That bothered her, and one time she even told me so. I wasn't trying to hurt her. I just had the theory that it wasn't my dad's fault that she wasn't there. And if I came to visit, why not spend time with him. He didn't like it either, though. Many, many times he would tell me that I needed to go spend time with her. He would encourage it. It was just hard for me to do. At this point, I should have been able to let it go. I just wouldn't. So I sat on those feelings and let them keep eating at me. They manifested into other feelings and honestly, before my accident, it was really bad. There were situations that had happened in my life that I was just so tired of dealing with. The more tired I got of those things, the worse my whole outlook got. That would rub off on other things. I was a cancer in my own life. It was impossible for me to find the good in any situation. I didn't trust anyone. Church was hard to swallow. I just began to spiral downward. There were times where I had thought about taking my own life. I know that sounds crazy. But if it weren't for my wife and son, I would have probably been a lot closer to that than I want to believe. That is a completely irrational thought. It is NEVER rational to think that way. I was just that deep into a hole. I fought the bad, and the good. Even if something great came along, I fought it. I didn't have any hope. I was constantly searching for something. I had lost all feeling of self-worth. The enemy had clearly used past circumstances to start destroying my life…and I was letting him. This was a very dark point in my life that a lot of people didn't even realize I was going through. I let a lot of people down. I hurt a lot of people. I'm truly sorry.

During those hard times before the accident, I met a friend who got me into cooking meat. I loved it. It gave me something to do and it cleared my mind of a lot of things. Regretfully, I lost touch with that friend. I was going through so much at the time. It hurt, and I probably wasn't the best of friend either. But I loved cooking meat and it was a great hobby. We had a lot of mutual friends and it seemed like we all kind of lost touch around the same time. We attended the same church and a situation arose and we all kind of decided to go different directions. It was probably at the worst time for me. Through all of that, I felt the most alone at that time. I was in serious need of something. I had a great wife and son, and I loved them dearly. More than anything. But emotionally I was done. The only feelings at the time I could muster up was for those two. On top of that, I didn't even feel worthy of being their father and husband. Irrational again, yes. But that's where my mind was. I told Meg that I needed to get away. Not leave the family but just go away for a weekend. I found a BBQ competition in Oklahoma and I wanted to give it a shot. She thought it was a good idea. I had competed with my friends in years past but this time was my first solo. I had tried my best to form new recipes and I can just remember needing SOMETHING to lift my spirits. So I took off and drove to that contest with a pop up canopy as my shelter. On the way to this competition I noticed an RV of sorts pulled over on the side of the interstate. It appeared as if they were pulling a BBQ smoker and it had blown a tire. There were about eight people standing around this thing and it was pouring down rain. I made mental note of it, but I thought "I'd pull over if there weren't eight people out there, I bet they have it covered." I was already running a little late to the competition so I headed on. I got to the competition, got checked in and set up, then waited. I had no one there to talk to. I was not doing well. I felt like I could just let go at any moment. I tried calling Dad and he calmed me down a little. I didn't know anyone. I was in the back corner of this place in a grassy field. It was beginning to seem like a bad decision. So I just went and sat in my old truck and tried to fall asleep. It was raining and I remember just sitting in that truck and crying. It was horrible. I felt like I was on the verge of a panic attack at any moment. After a bit, the rain let up and I told myself I needed to get out of the truck and start walking around. If I find someone, talk to them. Be happy. Act happy. Find a reason to be happy and make some friends. So I started walking. A lot of people were out and around, but I walked by and noticed that RV that was pulled over on the side of the road on my way there. I recognized the people because they had been nice enough to come help me put my canopy up before the weather got bad. I didn't realize they were the ones I left behind. So I got to talking to them. Introduced myself. They knew I was from Arkansas and I don't think they remembered my name, so I started joking with them and just trying to have fun. I'd make my laps and every time I'd pass them they'd scream "Arkansas!" It was fun and we had a good time. It was much needed. My new friends Kevin and Tabby were awesome and a much needed lift to my spirits. I didn't have a lot of confidence in the competition. There were a lot of great teams there and honestly, I just prayed I'd hear my name get called one time. They had trophies, but I knew the odds of someone like me taking one of those home was pretty much astronomical. Like Dad said, "Just do the best you can do, find time to relax, and see how you measure up." That's what I did. In the BBQ competition world, they announce the top ten places in each meat category. There are four meats including pork, ribs, chicken, and brisket. So just to hear your name get called as finishing in the top ten in a single meat category is a big deal… especially in this field of competition. I prayed and I worked hard. I honestly felt like I didn't deserve anything. But I knew I needed something to spark excitement in my life. Some form of encouragement. I knew brisket was my strong suit. Chicken being my weakest at the time. Ribs were decent and honestly, I didn't know what to expect with my pork entry. About the time my brisket was about thirty minutes from coming off the smoker, a huge storm hit. It was horrible. I was standing in six inches of water. My smoker fire had completely gone out. My brisket was as tough as a sirloin steak. That's not good for brisket. I figured that was my only hope. I didn't have time to put more wood in the fire. Most of it was wet anyway. I had tried my ribs and they were a little too tough for my liking. My chicken looked like Dax trimmed it and put it in the box for me. It was a complete mess. I remember picking out the best of what I thought was the worst ribs I had ever cooked to turn in. I walked by Kevin at his camp and he asked how I did. I told him my ribs were horrible. I was so disappointed I was almost in tears. I turned in all my meats and came back to my camp and I had accepted defeat already. Normal for me at that time. I didn't have hope in any circumstance. So why would I find any at a BBQ competition? So I meet up with Kevin and Tabby and we went to the awards portion. I didn't expect to hear anything, but I was rooting for my new friends. Chicken was up first and when eighth place rolled around, they actually called my name. I took a minute to respond because I was so shocked. There's no way they called on me for Dax's chicken, Ha! I was elated. No trophy, but it made my day. Next up was the rib category. One by one they called all the way down to fifth place. At fifth place they stared giving away trophies and in my mind I was thinking, "Yeah my best shot here would be six through tenth place. Not a chance with the good teams here." But on the fifth place call, they called my name. I got a trophy! And on the pork category, I got another fifth place call and another trophy! I'm not lying when I said my brisket was like a sirloin. There were no calls for brisket. But as for the others, I was in shock. I tried to play it off like I was not shocked, Ha! But inside, I was screaming. Kevin looked at me laughing and said, "Yeah those ribs were REAL bad huh?" I just simply replied, "Yeah they were." I had never been more proud of myself in my lifetime. For the first time in as long as I can remember, two fifth place trophies and an eighth place chicken gave me more hope than I had been able to conjure up in years. I pulled away from that competition, with a sixth place overall finish. All of the "pros" who competed every weekend were coming up to me asking who I was and how long I had been competing. They really wanted to know who I was! I didn't even know how to act. I just knew I was excited for once. I had new friends and something to give me hope. I put those two trophies right next to me in the truck. It was raining the whole way back to Arkansas, but I literally hugged them in my right arm as I drove home. I remember calling my dad on the way and telling him the news. He was crying for me. He knew how much it meant for me. I was so proud. I don't know that anyone in the world has been more proud of two fifth place trophies in their lives. I was nowhere near complete again, but God started showing me things then. I was a long ways away, and He had His work cut out for Him, but that single BBQ competition started me on a long term healing process. On the way home, I noticed Kevin and Tabby pulled over again. They had another flat tire. But I was tired and also excited. Those eight people were still there to help, and I kept driving. I feel really bad about that. As happy as I was, my mind was still in a rough spot and even after they helped me, the least I could have done was stop to attempt to help them. But it's ok, to this day, they still remind me that I didn't pull over to help all eight of them change one tire in the rain, Ha! I don't know if I'll ever hear the end of that one!

A few months later there was another competition at that location. I wanted to give it another try. I didn't fare as well at this one, but after meeting Kevin and Tabby at the first one, I didn't get their contact info. So I was glad to see they were back at the next. From then on we have remained in touch through the years and they have turned out to be some of my closest friends. There are people that I mention in this book. All of them special. All of them I firmly believe saved my life at some point in time. I've tried to express how dark of a time I was in when I met them, and until they read this, they still may not even know, but I know God put them in my life to get me through those times. I feel like I owe so much to them. They still come to help me cater events and just hang out. We talk cooking meat all the time! Every time something has happened in my life since then, they have been there for me. They need to know how much I love them and I thank them for saving me through a time, even if they don't even realize the magnitude of their place in my life. Maybe they do now.

As happy as that time was, and as much as I needed it, I still had a lot to make it through. I was still harboring anger and self-doubt and the enemy was using it against me at every moment. I knew I had to start mending things. I didn't know how, but I knew I had to try. About a month before my accident, my dad had an event at his church where he had a speaker come in and there was music…kind of like a modern day revival service. I know God was working on me there. My dad talked us brothers into singing a song for one of the services. It went well. But I felt like I wasn't worthy. Towards the end of the event, on about night three, my dad actually invited my mom to sing. See, my mom used to travel all over the country and sing with him. When he would preach services, she would sing. Stacey had passed. Dad was still getting over that, but it was time to continue healing. Mom had apologized and things were well on their way to healing. Dad asked me if I minded if he asked her to sing. I immediately told him I thought it would be a great idea. He said, "I don't know why, I just feel like she needs to sing." So she did. I sat back on the very back row of the church. Alone. Ashamed. Borderline embarrassed to even be there. My dad got up and actually introduced my mom to come and sing. It was surreal. But she got up and sang one of our favorite songs. I was all but in the floor in the back of that church. A flood of emotions rang through me. It was like old times. I felt so useless for God, but at the same time, I could clearly see God using my mom again. I could see that my dad was over it. He had moved on and opened a door that I, personally, couldn't open yet. Y'all, I was so emotional that people were staring at me. I couldn't hold it in. So I just got up and walked out mid song. I knew I had a pit in my stomach, I knew God was trying to get ahold of me, and now, instead of the anger I was harboring over the situation with my mom, He was using her to help heal me…and I couldn't begin to process that. So I ran. I walked out of the church in a sloppy mess, but I didn't want anyone else to see me. Shortly after I had to leave to go back to Northwest Arkansas. I caught her outside of my truck and I was a mess. I tried to apologize to her and I promised I was trying to fix it. She said I didn't have to apologize, but I still felt like I needed to. I had a lot of feelings that I was trying to get rid of. God was dealing with me for sure. A few more weeks went by, and that's where it all came to a head with the accident. That's where my mental state was when I had the accident. I was beginning to come around, but I wasn't there. I wasn't in a position to see clearly. I still didn't have the faith and hope that I needed. God knew it was going to take drastic measures to get me to the point where I needed to be for Him.

When I was transported from the woods to the helicopter, the last person I remember seeing as I got on the helicopter was my mom. That was reassuring. She took off two weeks and stayed and slept in the hospital with me when I got there. A lot of my recollection of that time is foggy, but I do know that she told me, "I've left you once before, I'm not going to leave you again." She stayed there and took care of me. I had not had a "Mom" like that in a long time and it was nice. I know my dad called to check on me at one point. He was up to visit almost every day. But one day when he called he said, "Son, I don't want you to be upset that I'm not there a lot right now, but I want your Mom to have a chance to take care of you. She needs this. I'm going to stay out of the way and let her have her time to take care of you. She's your mother, she deserves it." I respected that. Mom and I had a lot of healing moments both literally and figuratively. I talked earlier about having a notebook where I wrote down my "Why's." Reasons that I could have been put in this situation. One of them specifically says, "Restoring a loving relationship with my mom."

Since that time, I talk to my mom almost daily. I went months at points in my life without talking to her or even seeing her. But now, I'm afraid I even bug her at times. She says I don't, but I don't believe her, Ha! She even went and braved a BBQ competition with me. Which is crazy because we had to sleep in the truck. A storm blew through that night, which is something I'm just coming to grips with and expecting at every single competition I go to, but I know she hated that…but she was a trooper and pushed through it just to spend time with me. It didn't go unnoticed.

Before I go further in my life's journey, I want you all to know that again, harboring these negative feelings has no positive outcome. They only hurt you. One day God will fix it. He's not going to ask you what "fixing" process YOU prefer, either. But I encourage each and every one of you to restore the torn relationships with friends and family. It's not worth it. People make mistakes. Find a way to forgive them and move on. I kept so much anger hidden in me that it became toxic. There's never a reason for that. I love my mom and I'm so glad things are finally working out for the better. I'm glad God used this situation to restore that relationship.

# 8

## HEBREWS 13:2

Leaving the comfort of the hospital was a lot scarier than I thought it would be. As you've come to notice by now, you develop great relationships with people and the care I was given was beyond anything I can imagine. It was exciting knowing I was getting to go to Wayne's and recover. Before we left the hospital, they had arranged for a home health nurse to come in as well as physical therapy. I'll admit that I was naïve. I was convinced that I was on the mend. I did have mixed emotions because there was a huge part of me that didn't feel ready. I wanted to be able to be lifted off the bed with the Hoyer lift. We had only tried that one time at the hospital and it was scary. But that would help me do necessary things. At the time I thought it would be easy to just get up in that lift and get in a wheel chair and I'd just haul around Wayne's house and we'd have a great time while I recovered. That's what I thought. I would quickly find out that would not be the case…at all.

They came to take me from the hospital and I never

thought it would be as emotional as it was. Every nurse that had cared for me that had a shift in the hospital that day was present. I tear up thinking about it. I felt so supported and I would honestly miss every one of them. Because of the dizziness when I would sit up, they went ahead and transferred me to a stretcher to take me to an ambulance. Yes, the funny thing is I left the hospital the same way I came in. On a stretcher. We made our way out and through the basement of the hospital. The doors opened and I felt a rush of cold air hit my face and the smell....just the simple smell of fresh air. I took the biggest breath I've ever taken. For the first time in over five weeks, I could actually smell "outside" again. It felt so good. In an effort to not sound cliché, it did feel freeing. The things we take for granted.

Wayne's house was only around a thirty minute drive from the hospital so it wasn't too bad. The good news is we were still close if we needed to go back for an emergency. I had accumulated a few boxes of stuff and Meg had packed them. We had to get my medicine filled. That was a huge blow. My blood thinning medicine alone was over eight hundred dollars a month. I had the wound-vac that needed care and supplies. Luckily we had some left over from the hospital stay but those would soon run out again. There was a petroleum jelly coated gauze patch that was very helpful in the treatment of my skin graft donor sites as well as for the wounds themselves that turned out to be way harder to obtain than expected. It was a mess. They wheeled me in at Wayne's house, they had already cleared a room and put a hospital bed in it complete with a trapeze bar, which I loved. There was a Hoyer lift in there…but it was manual. The one at the hospital was this huge machine and it had no problem lifting my big self and probably one extra person if needed. This little thing didn't look like it would hold a dog...much less me. There was a TV in there and that was nice. I had Wayne put the fan on me because you know how I am with fans! And my nine hundred pillows made the trek too.

This first day was comforting. My mom had come back in town and was there for a day or two to get me transitioned. Wayne had put a chair in the room to come and watch TV with me until I fell asleep each night. It was calming, but stressful too. I wasn't a huge fan of giving myself shots for blood thinning. I had to get used to that. I had a steady dose of pain medicine and that helped. The wound-vac scared me to death. They checked that thing so many times at the hospital. It seemed like someone was in there every hour to make sure it was sucking and doing what it was supposed to do with a clean seal. Now I'm alone with no nurses present and it was really unnerving to know after all that checking, that somehow it was supposed to just randomly be ok now. I mean, I still had a huge gaping hole in my leg. The only thing protecting that was this extremely fragile plastic sheet with a straw coming out of it that was hooked up to some kind of vacuum that seemingly sucked the life and every ounce of fluid from my leg. Seemed legit. But I did what I was told and tried to not touch or worry about it. There would be a nurse coming in to take care of it...we hoped.

I can't stress to you how un-prepared I was to be there in that condition. I thought I was good. It was getting close to Christmas and I don't necessarily blame the hospital, but whoever was making the decision to actually send me home was already gone for Christmas vacation and whoever her substitute was made the final decision. Well, a doctor made a decision, and she approved it. In a way I understand. Its Christmas, the more patients that are there to take care of, the more staff that has to miss family time and actually come to work to take care of them. No one told me that. I'm not, in any way, attempting to throw anyone under the bus here. I just assume that's why I was sent home. That and I seemed to be on the mend. I just remember a random young doctor coming in, he was a med student, standing at the foot of my bed saying, "Yeah man you don't want to be here. It's Christmas. We're going to get you out of here." I remember looking at my mom like "Is he serious?" Actually, I was scared to death. I was not ready. I didn't really know what to do. So, we were initially told that I could go to a rehab facility, but then told they wouldn't accept me because I was only weight bearing on one limb and I needed to be more mobile to be admitted. So even requesting to be admitted to one of those facilities was pretty much deemed out of the question. The best bet for us, for being close for upcoming follow up appointments, was to stay at Wayne's house.

After a day or two at Wayne's I remember not eating much. I didn't eat a whole lot in the hospital either. Full disclosure here, because I want you to understand the stress that I was under, and I won't go into too many highly embarrassing details… but going to the bathroom was a challenge. I hated it. Enough said. Not to mention the heavy pain medicine I was taking and had been taking, helped prevent that…which is NOT a good thing. But my theory, whether correct or not, was the less I ate, the less that had to happen. That is not healthy. But neither is the stress of having to go through that process. God help us all. I remember Meg would bring me two or three slices of lunch meat and a piece or two of cheese and be almost in tears because that's all I wanted to eat. There were times she would get Dax to bring me food because she knew I would eat it if he brought it. Other than that, those first couple of days at Wayne's were pretty good. I was able to relax and it was nice to sit and watch TV with Dax most of the day. On about day three things started to change a little. I was happy to be around my family "full time," but things were really starting to get to me. The home health nurse, God bless her, was less than stellar. I say that in the nicest way. To her defense, maybe it wasn't that she was subpar, but rather that I had superior treatment from the nursing staff at the hospital. When this new one came in, God Bless her, I feel like I have to keep saying that, she started touching the wound vac. I could tell it made her nervous. Her first words were, as if that's literally the only thing she came to do for me that day, "Ok I need to change the dressing on this wound-vac."

Me: "Ok great! I think it needs it! Have you ever done this before?"

Y'all, by the look on her face, I knew the answer to my own question. It was facetiously hypothetical.

"Actually, no Mr. Preston, but I'm sure I can figure it out!"

Insert immediate patient vomiting here. Well I didn't really, but that comment made me sick to my stomach. I had watched trained professionals do this for weeks. If someone had a question, there was a white coat there to direct them. Every time the plastic surgeon walked into my room, before asking questions he simply grabbed supplies and re-packed and covered it. The good news is I had seen it done a million times.

So, you bet your bottom I was going to give her instructions. God Bless her. And I did. I wasn't mean to her. I just wanted to make sure it was done right. Doctors worked very hard to save that leg and I didn't want that to be jeopardized by someone not knowing how to properly care for it. It didn't help that she immediately started pulling the plastic off the wrong way. Nothing was pre-prepared to cover it back up as soon as possible. Which means she would have to completely sterilize herself in between and while my wound was sitting there exposed to whatever was in the air. I think the first couple of instructions upset her a little. After that, I reminded her that I had seen it done numerous times and if she would just allow me to walk her through it, we'd all be ok. So, she did. For all intents and purposes, I trained her how to maintain a wound-vac. Over the next few days she did become my friend and I appreciate everything she did for me. For the most part, she had to be there for a certain time each day, and she was a heck of a listener... but after that experience, unless I was back at the hospital, I pretty much took care of myself as much as I legally could.

While she was there for the first day, the physical therapist came in to evaluate me. He asked me to sit up on the side of the bed. Which I had only done maybe twice. When I did, I almost fell over. I was so dizzy. He said "Here Mr. Preston, grab my hand." I reached for the one in the middle. I saw about 4 of them. I missed. Almost fell on the floor. He caught me and it freaked him out. Rightfully so. He was also not too keen on the wound-vac either. I could tell he was well put together. He sat next to me on the bed and flat out told me I wasn't ready for physical therapy yet. Talk about a hard blow. "What do I do?" He said "I don't know, we'll have to talk to a doctor, but I don't know what I can do to help you here until they let you walk on your legs." That was heartbreaking. Any hope I had built up about getting out of that bed and at least riding around the house in a wheel chair, or going to the bathroom "normally," was shattered. I hit a very low point right then. The reality that I would be lying on my back at Wayne's house for the next twelve weeks, after I had convinced myself that I had conquered the gauntlet of being immobile for five previous weeks, was slapping me right in the face. It wasn't pretty. I remember thinking about twelve weeks. Then the more I thought about it, I started doing the math, and as soon as my mind wrapped around the hard truth that I would be in that bed, immobile, on my back for over twice as long as I had already been in the hospital…Y'all the panic and anxiety was unbearable. I was on medication to help this, but it wasn't working. It wasn't even touching it. I was malnourished, granted by my own doing, weak, not confident in my care staff, in pain, my intestinal "pipes" were backed up, and it was just the perfect storm. I felt so sorry for Wayne. Poor Meg was pregnant so she needed rest. Kristi was watching Dax most of the time. But like clockwork, Wayne would come in and sit in a chair by the bed and watch basketball with me until I literally cried myself to sleep. I needed help. I tried praying. I tried to find peace. I couldn't. I just couldn't.

A day later I was in the bed. Wayne was at work and Meg had gone to run some errands. Kristi was around the house. I wasn't alone. But all I remember is someone coming in the room. She had a very sweet spirit about her. She didn't look nervous. It was actually calming. I was literally fending off panic attacks every second. She walks in, no name tag. The other people wore name tags. She didn't have one, nor was she in scrubs. I didn't get alarmed, but they are things I noticed. You know me! I observe and react. She calmly said, "Hey, I'm Ms. Betsy, I'm here to give you a bath today!"

"Wow that sounds great!" I said, "I need one."

"I bet you do!"

I noticed she didn't bring anything with her. Nothing. No supplies for bath giving. No soap. Not a single thing. I pointed over to a box by the closet and told her I had things from the hospital and there should be some leftover bath things in there. So, she grabbed them and came to lay them on the bed next to me. She then walked out of the room and went straight to a closet and grabbed a towel or two. This was odd to me. She doesn't live here. How did she know where to go for that? Like it was her own house. It didn't startle me, I just took mental note. She came back in and here's where things got a little crazy. "Hutch" is a nickname given to me at the time of my birth. My mom's maiden name is Hutcheson and my grandfather, a veteran, was called "Hutch" in the military. So, I was specifically named "Hutcheson" for that reason…to be called "Hutch." Having said that, "Hutcheson" is my middle name. I have a legal first name that everyone in the medical field called me until they officially met me. As a matter of fact, if you call me by my first name, I know immediately that you don't "know" me. Which means if you call me "Hutch," we've been introduced, or you truly know me. Now that's a long explanation, I get it. But obviously everyone else who came in that room called me by my first name. It then transitioned to "Mr. Preston." And that's where this story takes a turn.

She came up to the bed and started the process of giving

the bath. Baths usually consisted of a small tub of water with some form of medical grade soap and a wash cloth. Essentially a sponge bath. She was an African American lady. As she bathed me, she stared humming the most soulful medley of Hymns. She's humming "How Great Thou Art." I just closed my eyes and lost it. Tears everywhere, snot. It was bad. She stops humming for a moment and as my eyes were closed and still crying asked how I got my injuries. I shortly explained. She then replied, "You're a lucky man."

"I know, I could be dead."

"No, you're lucky because God loves you. If God decided not to take you home then He has big plans for you."

It seemed impossible, but I started crying even more. "Who is this lady?"

"Hutch, why are you crying?"

I'm startled. She just called me Hutch. That's impossible. I'm completely shocked and she knows it. I can see it in her eyes. It's almost like she knows I know, you know? I haven't put it all together yet but it's definitely fishy. As I'm staring at her, she just kind of grins and says,

"If only you knew how much God loves you."

And she said this like she knows. Like I'm the only person on the planet that can't grasp it.

"You're His Child. He never intended for you to be discouraged. Keep your mind on the positive blessings He's given you."

I felt like I was floating. I can't explain it. She asked if she could pray with me. I closed my eyes and she put her hand on my shoulder. I've never heard a prayer like that. I've heard many of them. But I've never heard someone pray like THAT before. Ever. It was on a whole different level. I'm ashamed that I don't know that I've ever been engulfed in God enough to have the knowledge and fortitude to utter such words. I'm not "Churching" this up either. It was the real deal.

When she was done praying she packed everything up and came back over to the bed. Looked at me, smiled, and said "Never, ever forget the love God has for you." And she went on her way. Later that evening my home nurse came in and I mentioned it to her. My at home nurse had no record of anyone ordering a bath for me that day. She had also never heard of anyone named "Ms. Betsy."

Maybe someone ordered a bath. Maybe there just wasn't a record. Maybe no one knew who she was. Maybe it was all just coincidence. The fact remains that she was there. It was real. The conversation and experience was real. And most incriminating of all...she called me "Hutch." How did she know that? I could sit here and try to come up with excuses all day. I refuse to. Whatever may be, in that moment, God sent her to me. Whether human, or angel, only God knows how much I needed that. The experience was all too real. If there was any doubt about what I saw in the woods the day of my accident...maybe I was hallucinating...well, I can guarantee I was NOT hallucinating on this day. I'm realizing God is showing me something. He's still not finished.

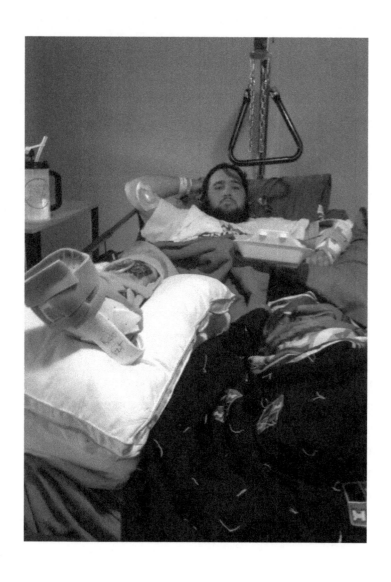

# 9

# REHABILITATION

By the time I made it to the rehabilitation center, I was beginning to fall back into some of the dark places in my mind. I was tired. I was malnourished, granted by my own choice, and I had such great care at the hospital, that I was really nervous about what would be next. I had not gone any "number" in a normal bathroom in weeks. You'd be surprised how much of a toll that will take on your psyche. The professional nursing care at Wayne's house was really not what I was used to or had expected it to be when I got there. It was right before Christmas and apparently there is a large turnover with staff in those facilities. I didn't know that. When making arrangements to get into that specific rehab, we knew we wanted a private room. With Meg being pregnant and us having a three-year-old Dax, we thought the best way to get through this was to have somewhere to ourselves. I needed to see them every day. From what I knew, it was agreed to that we'd have a private room for the duration of the stay. This whole process was a learning experience and healing time for me. Not just physically, but spiritually. I was being fought with anxiety and panic at every

turn. Even with my special visitor at Wayne's house (yes, I had
those things to hold on to) but I was still being fought with
other distractions and worries. Plus, it's an actual medical
disorder. So, with all of the medications I was taking, between
pain medicine, some of my other medications being adjusted,
and not realizing that my anxiety medication was actually
changed, it's really a wonder I wasn't worse than I was. To top
that all off, here I was uncomfortable, in a place that I'm
unfamiliar with…alone. I remember Cliff came up and spent
the night in the empty bed in the room so I could have some
company. The next morning, we were told he wasn't allowed to
do that. That was frustrating. Now I'm alone in this place
where I don't know anyone, and after a certain time in the
evening, I'm pretty much locked in there. I couldn't move, I
was just lying on my back. It was a terrifying time for me.
There was one RN for the whole wing. There were CNA's that
would come and do vital checks. They were nice, and I tried to
get to know them. But after a few days and starting to feel
comfortable, they would be gone and replaced with someone
else. I remember one guy came in and he was great. I could
talk to him and he really helped ease my mind. I began to think,
"You know, I can make it with this guy here." I finally got
comfortable and if I was feeling rough, I could tell him and he'd
take care of it. I felt at peace knowing he was just in the
building. Then one evening a random guy walked in with my
medicine. He was the new RN. Later a CNA that I had kind of
developed a relationship with came in and I said, "Where is
J.C.?" She said, "He no longer works here." Within a two-
week period, every single staff person that I met, with the
exception of that one CNA, had left that facility. I didn't know
that was common. All I knew is that occasionally there would
be a CNA come through to check vitals, that would be wiping

tears and visibly emotional. Occasionally I could hear them talking to each other complaining about something that had happened. Then they were all gone. I was so uncomfortable with a few of them, that even though they said they HAD to administer my blood thinning shot, I wouldn't let them. I insisted that I do it myself… and I did. Those first two weeks were some of the most stressful times there.

About two days into my stay there, two ladies came in and I had not seen them before. I had a few physical therapists come through, but they didn't work there full time. They were fill-ins because of the holiday season. I remember when Amanda and Lisa came in, it caught me off guard because they were actually smiling and it calmed me down. They told me they were the physical therapists for the place and they seemed really down to earth and not stressed out at all. It was actually really calming. They did a preliminary assessment and said they would go get a plan to start working on me. They next day they came back in and said that I was just not ready for physical therapy and they'd have to wait until I was actually released to do physical activity by my doctor. I didn't see them again for two weeks. I didn't know they were leaving to go on their Christmas break vacation time. I just know they disappeared. As I said, during those two weeks, everyone but one CNA that I had met was gone. It was a revolving door. That uncertainty, coupled with crying CNA's, and the only people at the time that I felt comfortable around were now missing, and that was just nauseating. I had about two weeks where I just went into a huge fog of doubt and honestly just numbness. I wanted someone to come stay and talk with me. My brothers would come up. Dad would see me. But soon they'd leave. Meg would bring Dax up for the day, but she was tired from pregnancy and I felt guilty for even asking her to make the trip over to spend time there. There were a few things I would eat, but I wouldn't eat much. I had lost sixty-five pounds to that point from the accident. I know that because when I was in a Hoyer lift, they were able to weigh me. It got pretty downright exhausting. I couldn't let myself fall back into the trap of doubt and fear. I started watching preachers on TV. I tried reading my Bible. I tried everything I could do to stay positive and keep my mind clear. I asked Meg to bring me a drawing pad and a notebook to write in. When that got old, I'd move on to something else. My attitude was turning sour, but I was trying everything I could. My bed was right next to the window. I could see Interstate 30 and cars passing by only about a hundred yards from my window. Y'all, I literally started counting cars that would pass by on the interstate. For over a week, that's what I did to pass my time and get my mind off of things to fight off doubt and depression. I was determined to make it through this. Keep in mind that I can't move from that spot unless someone comes and physically moves me. I'm lying on my back for weeks and I still would for weeks to come. At that time, I had been on my back for more than six weeks and I still had to fight through at least twelve more that I already knew of. There were more to come, I just didn't know that yet and I'm thankful I didn't.

So, I'm lying there spending my day counting cars. I took my writing notebook and it would be full of tally marks. I would share my statistics but I'm not completely sure what happened to that notebook. After a day or so, I was amazed at how many cars passed by on that interstate. So, then I went from keeping up with how many cars would pass during certain times of the day. Day after day I would get an average of how many would come during morning rush hour, then lunch time, then afternoon rush. I started distinguishing between semi-trucks, vans, utility vehicles and so forth. You'd be surprised. When that got old, I started counting red cars only. Then blue ones. Then black. That's what I did to keep my mind occupied. I remember I could see the door to the wing I was in. The one from the outside in. I could watch people walk from the parking lot to the door, then I would count how many seconds it would take them to pass my doorway. My door was always open, so then I would count and see how many of those people curiously peaked in on their way by. And on the good days, the great days, I would see Meg and a hopping Dax walking up that sidewalk and I would be so excited to see someone, especially them, that I would just be an emotional wreck when I laid eyes on them. For all of my family and friends that came to visit me, you have no idea how much it meant for you to be there.

Another one of my best friends from college is Jamey. By appearance, Jamey would pass as my brother. When he would leave, many people would think one of my brothers came to visit. Jamey is originally from Oklahoma but relocated to central Arkansas with his job. He happened to live within only a few minutes from the rehab facility. I'm telling you, you know who your true friends are during times like these. Jamey would come sit and talk with me. Watch TV. Best yet, he would bring me real food that I felt like eating. Mostly BBQ. When things started to take turns for the worse, Jamey just magically showed up at the perfect times. It seemed every time I was about to start falling towards the bottom, Jamey would call and say, "Hey Dude! I'm on my way! What do you want to eat?" It was perfect timing. When car counting just wasn't cutting it... Jamey showed up. Jamey will never understand the impact he had on my recovery. I truly hope he realizes how God used him to help me.

Still within that first two-week time period, Christmas rolled around. We always have a big family Christmas gathering with my dad's family on Christmas Eve. I hated missing it. Dad made the two-hour drive and sat with me during the day on Christmas Eve before he drove back to be with family that evening. That was a special day. It was always calming to have him there. We'd talk, but most of all, he always prayed with us. I'll never forget those prayer times we had while I was in that rehab. He knew I was struggling and I could see that he was worried. I tried my best to keep a strong appearance but it didn't work. Mom would also come up as much as she could. Uncle Larry would usually come with Dad. I know he worried about me. I felt so horrible because I know he thought this was all his fault. I've tried so hard to convince him it's not. It never was.

On Christmas Day, Meg brought Dax up and I remember she had a ginger bread house kit for us to build together. Santa Clause actually came to the rehab room I was in and surprised Dax with his gifts that morning. We had fun. We watched Christmas movies all day, Dax snuggled up in the bed with me and we drew ninja turtles and when the day was over, I remember telling Meg how much fun I had. It was simple. There was no one else there but us. We practically locked ourselves in a room and had the best Christmas I've had in a long time. It definitely lifted my spirits for a few days. I didn't have a lot of energy during the days. If I didn't get naps in I would be worn completely out by dusk. I remember not even really having time to be sad that they left for the day, because I fell right to sleep when they did. That Christmas Day was special.

Shortly after Christmas I had another surgery. They needed to go in and try to re-apply the skin graft. I had laid on my back for so long, that sitting up left me dizzy and I couldn't gain my sense of direction. When I would sit up, the whole room would spin, I would get nauseated, it was horrible. By spin, I mean, it was unbearable. This was the first time I would be transported from the rehab facility to the hospital for any kind of surgery or appointment. There was no way I could just get in a regular wheel chair...I would have passed out. So, they found some type of wheel chair-type-bed-slash-cot... I'm really not sure what it was called, but they were able to get a Hoyer lift in and transfer me from that bed to that special wheelchair that left me lying back enough to keep my equilibrium in check. It was really uncomfortable, but at least I wasn't dizzy and nauseated. I had to be at the hospital very early. So, we got there and went through the surgery procedures. By that afternoon I was released and I had to make sure I was picked back up to go back to the rehab facility. Somehow in the process, the transport driver got lost or delayed doing something, so after major surgery, I'm in pain. I laid down in the lobby of that hospital stuck in that fancy chair for over an hour until they came to get me. By the time she got there, she was very apologetic and I appreciated it. I could tell it wasn't directly her fault but it was just something else to add to the wonders of getting adjusted there. When I got back to the facility, the driver left me in my room. Staff was notified that I was back, but staff had already changed for the afternoon/evening shift. There was only one staff person there that was qualified to use the Hoyer lift, and the facility had a policy that there had to be two certified Hoyer specialists in the room to operate the lift for safety reasons. Not to mention, during the staff changes, they were shorthanded. I laid in that chair for more than four hours. I fell asleep out of sheer exhaustion. Sometime after the four-hour mark, someone came in and woke me up. It was a therapist I had never met. One of the floating ones that would just show up because I was on their schedule. Apparently, I had therapy scheduled that day. I tried to tell her I just had surgery…that morning. She wasn't having it. So, she wheeled me down to the therapy room, made that chair sit upright, I was about to pass out and I kept telling her, but I did arm exercises with my good arm for thirty minutes while she sat there and watched. This is no exaggeration. I'm serious. Imagine you are on that merry go round in elementary school. Little Johnny is running around in circles spinning that thing like there was no tomorrow. Now grab a three-pound weight, sit in the middle of that merry go round, and try to successfully exercise with said weight. That was my experience. True story. I'm sure there is a medical term for this phenomenon…I don't currently have it. Regardless, I kept telling her the whole time that I didn't think it was smart for this to be happening. She kept telling me that "They" didn't like for patients to refuse therapy. I didn't know who "They" were but I was confident "They" wouldn't approve of what was going on. I mean, the lady was just doing her job. I just don't know where the logic was on that one. I had been under general anesthesia, sitting for over four hours in an extremely uncomfortable wheelchair that's sole purpose was to keep me lying down. Now I'm sitting up and doing mini dumbbell exercises whilst feeling as if I'm spinning at NASA being tested to see how long I can withstand g-forces. If I had the energy, I would have argued. When we were done, she laid me back down, pushed me to my room, and left. A while later, the CNA who was on duty that evening, who was now my friend, was literally in tears because I was still in that chair. She couldn't do anything about it. Finally, she just called another CNA to come help her. I kept trying to reassure her that I was ok. I was not ok. Not even close. But it wasn't her fault and I didn't want her risking her job just to get me in bed. Eventually, they were finally able to get me transferred and by that time it was dark. I don't even know what time it was. But, needless to say, I fell right to sleep.

After Christmas and the new year had rung in, that two-week time period was coming to a close. I was still on edge because staff changes were crazy. I didn't know who was who, and wouldn't allow myself to get attached to anyone because I knew if I did, they'd probably be gone in a few days anyway. I was definitely not a bundle of joy. People would come in and try therapy, but it was limited to tossing a rubber ball back and forth and squeezing some silly putty in my hand. Once someone put some beads in the silly putty and they said I had to pick all of those beads out of the silly putty. That was horrible. I'd have rather counted cars! Then one day I hear someone come in the door and it was Amanda and Lisa coming to check on me. I know that I wasn't in good spirits. I was probably downright rude to them. I was glad to see them, don't get me wrong, but counting thousands of cars had taken its toll. I was frustrated. I remember asking how secure their jobs were at the facility. They looked at me like they didn't understand. I finally just looked at Lisa. I knew she could see my discouragement. I said, "Lisa, where have you been?"

"I've been on vacation."

"Good…it's been a couple of weeks, right?"

"Something like that?"

"Good…Good… So, do you remember the last day you were here to see me?"

"I do!"

"Ok great… now if both of you will think of everything you've done since that time. Travel. See your family. All the Christmas presents you opened…think of everything you've done since that day around two weeks ago when you last saw me. Out of all of that stuff that happened in your life over the past couple of weeks, while it happened, I've been laying right here…staring out that window. From the day you left, until right now, I've been right here…my rear end still in this exact spot… think about that. I'm sorry if I'm coming across as a little off…but that's where I'm at, and what I'm dealing with. I've watched person, after person, after person come in that room, I'd get attached to them… then they'd be gone. Some of them crying on their way out for whatever reason. It's been miserable. It's not your fault. I've had a lot going on, but it's been miserable."

I could see the look on her face and it was a genuine, or at least seemed to me to be a sincere look of, "Oh my goodness, that's horrible… I can't imagine." It obviously clicked. So for the next little bit, they both stayed in there and explained the situation of being there, why there was a revolving door of staff, and what I could expect. They told me that from this day forward, the staff would pretty much stay the same because of the new year and they would make sure I was treated properly.

That really meant a lot to me. It brought me some much needed comfort. They still weren't able to work on me physically, but just now knowing the process and how everything was going to work, really encouraged me. Even though that group of therapists couldn't treat me yet, they all made a point to come and check on me...and that meant the world to me. Every single one of them probably thought I was crazy and off my rocker, and they had every right to at this point, but they at least seemed sympathetic to my situation and it really gave me a lot of comfort. I don't want to give the impression that this facility was some evil place. You have to realize there were a lot of variables that lead to my situations there. Things for me would get a little worse before they got better, but I need you to know that the staff at this place is amazing. Things weren't convenient for me and there was a lot going on. I probably treated some of them just as horribly as I felt and I sincerely apologize for that. Hopefully in the end, I made up for it.

I had a scheduled surgery for January 3rd. I remember that vividly because we had already met our insurance deductible and out of pocket max from my accident...and within three days of the new year, we had met it again. They were having to do a lot to the open wound on my leg. They tried the cow collagen procedure on my leg to close it up, but it didn't work. In fact, it failed miserably. A big reason for the majority of my scarring is from that failing. It's ok, I didn't really care all too much, but that's the reason. I lost a lot of tissue to what they called "sluffage." Yes, that sounds horrible, and that's because it is. Apparently, that's the term they used when skin tissue around my wound would die off and they would basically keep having to peel it away. Some of that was due to the constant "pressure washing" they did every other day in surgery to keep it clean and make sure all of those mud and dirt particles from that puddle I fell in were gone. Eventually, because of the location of that wound, they didn't have enough muscle tissue to do a regular skin graft on my leg to cover it...so they had to do some rearranging. They essentially went around the back of my calf muscle and cut one of the strands of muscle tissue. The soleus muscle. They then took a piece of my skin from my leg and wrapped it around to one side, then took that cut piece of calf muscle, and wrapped it around to the front, attached it to bone somehow, and used that tissue to graft on. I cannot begin to tell you how high on the pain scale that took me. That was probably the single most painful surgery and recovery that I had out of the ten surgeries to date. There was something about cutting that muscle that just ate me alive. There was no amount of pain medication that would touch that one for a few days. So, on January 3rd I had to go back in and have them look at that wound and close it up for good. Again, I was tired and mentally exhausted. They transported me from the rehab to the hospital via ambulance. I knew all of the pre-op staff in UAMS by now as well as every anesthesiologist they had on staff and in class there. They wheeled me in pre-op and I gave them my traditional three personal rules:

1. "I need one of those shots in my IV that makes me loopy and calm down. "Happy Shots," is what they were referred to."
2. "Because of severe pain, I realize I am a very large man, but will you please put me to sleep in this bed, then transfer me to the surgery table after I'm asleep? I know that will be difficult to do because of my size, and take eight people and maybe even a mule, but since I'm

already asleep I won't feel it…nor will I hear any names that you may call me in anger due to this process."

3. "For the love of everything holy…if you have to put a catheter in me, please, please, please, put that thing in after I'm asleep, and pull that sucker out before you wake me up."

If they followed those simple rules, which I personally didn't think was too much to ask, then we'd be all good. Now, the only one I could actually confirm they adhered to was the happy shots. But then again, once I got the happy shot, I really didn't care what else they did to me at that point.

Dad and Uncle Larry came up for this surgery. Meg was so close to having a baby, that we made her stay back and rest. It was comforting to know Dad was there with my uncle. I remember sitting in that pre-op room, Dad and my uncle to my right. Rehab had gotten a little easier to stomach, but I was still emotionally and physically exhausted. I remember I posted quite a bit on social media. Most of which was encouraging. What you don't realize is those were the things I was having to tell myself just to keep my head above the water. There just seemed to be a million and one things all hitting me at one time. I laid there in that room and Dad sat next to me. I just started crying. I tried to stay strong. I didn't want my uncle to see me suffering or appearing to be anything but happy. I didn't want him feeling like he put me in that situation. I was just at that breaking point. But just like all of the other times, when I was about to hit the bottom…someone else was there to pick me up. Dad prayed again, and we went on through with the surgery as always. This was a critical surgery. I just remember telling Dad that I needed this graft to work. I just needed it to stick.

The more it didn't stick, the further I would be from being able to bear weight on my legs when the bones were healed. I needed it to be fixed for good.

The surgery went well, but it went on into the evening. I was placed in a room for observation before they released me. While in the recovery area immediately after surgery. My friends had Sprite waiting for me as usual. My plastic surgeon wanted to keep me for the night. I was coherent enough to hear the conversation when the recovery room nurse was discussing me with another nurse about where they needed to put me. I just mumbled "F-9." They started laughing and the nurse said, "Is that where you'd prefer to go?"

"Yes, Please!"

"Well I'll give them a call and see if they have room for you."

I could hear her talking on the phone and I knew they said yes. She got off and said, "They said they would be glad to have you back!" Nine hundred pounds of stress and anxiety seemed to have lifted off my chest at that moment. I had confidence I'd be in good hands. I was so excited to finally get some stress-free sleep again. When recovery released me, they transferred me up to the floor. Y'all, thinking about it still makes me tear up, but every nurse that I can remember having during my time seemed to be at that door waiting for me to arrive. It was like a great reunion. You wouldn't think someone would be so excited about being back in a hospital room, but I was so relieved! I knew I was in great hands!

I had a great relationship with my plastic surgeon. To sum up his sense of humor, well, let's just say it meshed very well with my own. Then again, I may have been the only one who found his dry humor funny…and that's all that matters. He was honest when he first met me. I appreciated that. He said, "I'm really good at plastic surgery."

"Well that's good to know!"

"I figured you'd say that… but although my specialty is in reconstruction, it's primarily reconstruction for patients who have had breast cancer and need new ones. Seeing that you would probably prefer NOT to have new ones, I'll just fix your leg. You cool with that?"

How that was funny to me, like really funny, and not completely frightening is still beyond me. But I knew then that I was going to be ok with him. I knew he had a good reputation and I know my surgeries made him nervous, but I also knew he had the confidence to fix me.

As crazy as that story was, I apparently gave off the vibe that I was pretty laid back. Usually I am. As I said before, I had developed a pretty good relationship with him. My advice to anyone in my situation, that's probably a smart thing to do. He was a cool guy, though. He made it fun and it took a lot of the edge off. So, they would take skin for grafts from my upper thigh. I didn't know this until I got back to my room after the first time they did this. He came in and I remember itching down on that site. I had heard horror stories about how much those things hurt, but I honestly didn't even know they had taken any until he came in to check on them. Now that could have still been from the level ten pain I was going through from the hunk of calf muscle he cut to wrap around to the front of my leg to have tissue to graft to, but I like to think it was his newly experimental procedure… at least that's what he wittingly claimed. There was this petroleum jelly-soaked gauze that he would place on the fresh skin graft. Somehow that jelly kept the newly exposed skin moist while it healed. A lot of the pain from grafts come when that skin is trying to heal but later dries out… at least that's what they told me. After about a week, that gauze would dry up on its own, but as it dried, it kind of self-peeled away and by the time it peeled, underneath was pretty much healed…or at least healed enough to not hurt at all. I had a few donor sites. Honestly, I never felt the slightest pain. On the first time he did the procedure, this was explained to me after the fact. He came in to check them out and said "Yeah I need to get those staples out." I looked down, I had no idea I had gauze on my leg, much less approximately twenty staples holding this patch on. It literally looked like he didn't have a way to confirm the patch would stay on, and he just stapled it to my leg. So, I asked. That's exactly what happened. He was a little more amused about it than I was. I said, "So are that many staples necessary for that procedure?" His response? "Nope, but you were asleep, and I needed something to fasten the patch down, and the stapler was right over there… I didn't figure you would care." He was right, and that was hilarious to me. So, he pulled twenty plus, haphazardly placed staples out of my leg now that the patch was set and stuck. It was an experience to say the least. So that's who we were dealing with.

So, after this surgery and I was reunited with the staff that I missed dearly, he came up to check on me. It was just us in the room. He said, "Where are you at right now?"

"In a hospital room?"

"No, like where are you at? When you leave here, where are you going?"

"Oh, I'm in a rehabilitation center."

"Like a nursing home?"

"I mean, I guess… kind of?"

"That's what I thought. You hate it, don't you?"

"I mean…it's not the best right now, no."

"Good… that's why you're here. I figured you didn't want to go back there until you had to. I'll see you late tomorrow…you'll be fine. This one's going to heal fine."


That was so relieving. It was a blessing to know someone was looking out for me. Y'all I slept so well that night. The next day I felt like I was back to my old habits in the hospital. I was joyful. I had my friends back. I stayed by myself in that room and just looked out the window for once and I didn't count a single car! It was great. That evening the plastic surgeon came back in and he checked my wound out. "Yeah that's looking way better… you don't want to go back there tonight do you?" I just stared there at him knowing I didn't want to go back, but I also didn't want to push my limits. Before I could answer he said, "Well, good, I'm keeping you one more night. Congrats. Sleep well." So, I got two great nights. It was wonderful. That really perked me up!

I finally got discharged from that hospital stay and headed back to the rehab facility. I was nervous, but I felt rested and looking back on it, maybe rest and nourishment was my biggest issue. I still had some anxiety, but I was doing well. So, when I got back, I was met by the director of the facility. I didn't know what was going on. At the very beginning, when they told us they had a spot for us, we requested the single private room. We were led to believe that would be the scenario. We got there only to find out it wasn't. There had been another patient moved in to my room during that first two-week transition period. So, when this time the director was waiting for me, I was sure there was another patient about to be moved into my room. Instead, she was there to show me my new private room. It was a surprise. They had taken all my stuff and moved it over. That just made my day even better. A lot of my anxiety of being there was having a complete stranger in the room with me and not being able to get my family in there to spend time with me. So, this was a great thing. Things were starting to turn around for me. I laid in my new bed, on the opposite side of the facility, looked out the window, and all I saw was a bird feeder and grass. No interstate. No cars to count. Those birds were my new friends for the time being and that was a lot better. I could stare out that window and start to feel God again. You probably think this is just a roller coaster ride. It was. That's exactly right. I would see God...then seem to lose sight. Then I could get a glimpse of Him again, then back down. But I realized this was just the enemy fighting something good that was about to happen in my life. It was coming. I just had to keep fighting.

A few days later I was able to be transferred to the hospital for Dyar's birth. I was told if I would just keep lifting my head up a little more at a time, over the course of a couple of days, my body would regain whatever it had lost, and adjust back to being upright again. So that's what I did. When the time came for me to be going to the hospital for the scheduled birth, I was able to sit in a real wheelchair and enjoy it. We had to get up early, and Mom came up to be with us. It was a great time. The hospital staff wheeled me in the surgery room with Meg and I was able to take part in that. I sat over in the corner and heard that baby boy cry for the first time. I know I keep saying, "I lost it," and "I was a mess," but they're all true. I had a lot of crying moments during this adventure. But when you're so close to losing everything, and you hear that brand-new life coming into the world… Y'all there is nothing sweeter than a newborn baby breathing life for the first time. One of the rotating therapist had left a stretch band tied to my rehab bed. It was to help strengthen my good arm. I had finally been released a few days before to bear up to ten pounds with my broken arm. I wasn't fully weight bearing. So, I couldn't do a lot… but in secret each night in my rehab bed, I would work that bad arm with that stretch band. Maybe it wasn't the smartest of ideas. But it gave me a goal. I wanted to hold that baby with my broken arm. So, when that nurse brought him to me, I reached out that skinny, scarred up arm, and held all seven, crying pounds of him. I was so proud. This was a new beginning.

The nurse came and moved us to recovery. Another nurse came to ask us a few questions. I remember her saying, "Ok and who is the father?" I was like, "Yo! Right here!" I was so happy I was able to spend that time there. Just then, next to us was another lady. We were only separated by a curtain. I could hear her whispering to her new baby. She was alone in there. The nurse left us and went to her. I clearly heard her ask the same questions. When it came to, "Ok and who's the father?"

A soft motherly voice replied, "He doesn't have one." It broke my heart. I don't know why the baby didn't have a father. It's none of my business. But again, I just buckled with emotions. The reality of how close Meg was to sitting there and having to answer that question the same way this other poor lady had to, just punched me right in the gut. I decided then that I was ready to be a dad again. I was going to fight hard to rehab and get out of that place. Whatever I could do to get back to taking care of Meg, Dax, and now Dyar. One thing I can say is I don't feel like I ever let those past emotions before the accident affect my ability to be a father. I never got that far with them. Was I well on my way? Possibly. Maybe that's why God stopped it? I don't know. But I know now that I wasn't going to let anything stop me from this point forward. I went back to that facility and climbed in that bed. I started praying and doing everything I could to keep positive. Keep focused. I still had a few weeks left before I could bear weight on my legs, but I had to do what I could do to be prepared for it. The enemy still tried to fight. I got lonely. Meg had to take care of the baby and she would come up, but then leave again. It was sad. But I had to work hard at holding it together. I would feel like I was letting her down by not being there to help, but I knew if I worked hard, I could do it. It was just a matter of time. After a few more weeks of bed, I finally went back to the orthopedist for a check-up. My wounds were healing nicely. When I was leaving, I wasn't cleared to bear weight on my legs, but he did say I could start fully using the once broken arm. I said, "Like do anything?" He said, "Oh yeah, it's stronger than ever." If I could have run, I would have run out of there that day. It was a change. Another step in recovery.

I got back to the rehab facility and informed the therapists that I could fully use my arm. Lisa and Amanda came in the next day ready to go with a new therapist named Tandi. They were going to teach me to slide into a wheel chair from the bed. A feat they said would take a week to accomplish correctly. But once I could get in there, I would be mobile on my own. So, they'd put a board under me that created a bridge from the bed to the wheelchair. I would position myself onto the board and slide across the board to my short, desired destination. Eventually, I would learn to go from bed to chair, and chair back to bed. Now, I had been eyeballing that bathroom for weeks. I mean weeks! I just wanted a normal bathroom. I know it sounds crazy. But honestly try the alternative for a few weeks... you'll see what I'm talking about. I looked at them. With a stern look, and said, "I think I have this figured out."

"Oh yeah? Well let's not push ourselves too fast."

"Naw, I can make it... tell you what, you stand there, and you stand there and catch me, but if I can make it from this bed to that chair on the first try, will you take me to that bathroom and teach me there too?'

"Well, I suppose, but don't get your hopes up!"

Y'all, when she said, "I suppose," I grabbed that chair with my good arm and pulled myself right on to that wheelchair like I had done it a million and four times. They just kind of looked at me surprised and kind of excited and said, "Well I guess we'll get you into that bathroom!" It may sound a little odd, and I promise, it's more awkward for me to tell you this part of my life than it is for you to read it, but I was able to get in and out of that bathroom and in all seriousness, it was a turning point in my healing process. Have you ever seen that dog go to the

bathroom and run in circles for twenty-seven minutes? I know
what that dog feels like! Sixteen plus weeks of my life without a
real bathroom, Y'all! I think it was the last time I cried in rehab.
Well probably not the last, but the last mixed with a little
sadness. There was some embarrassment involved, but
still…my friend Jamey claims my whole outlook on life seemed
to change that day. He's probably right.

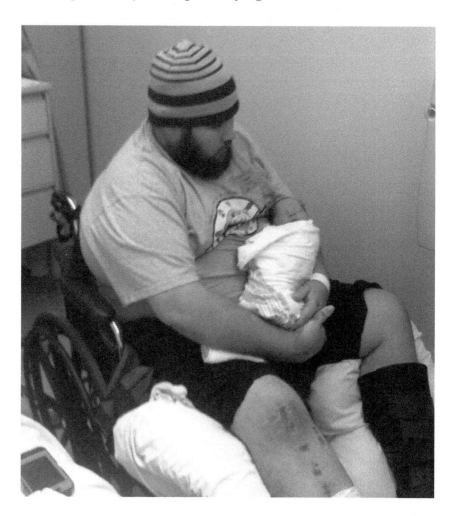

# 10

## MOBILITY

Mobility was a game changer. I mean a GAME CHANGER! I was finally able to form a routine. I'd wake up in the morning. Read my Bible. Have a quiet time. Transfer to my wheel chair and wheel myself to the bathroom. Brush my teeth in a real sink. It was great. From there I explored the building. I had been in there for weeks at this point, yet I had not even seen every room in the wing. I knew people were eating in a dining room area, but I could only imagine what it looked like. Now I was able to wheel myself in and check it out for myself. This place that I was so scared of at one time, was now not near as bad as I had once feared. People were nice! They spoke to me! There was consistency. It was everything they told me it would be!

I knew it was only a matter of time before I would be weight bearing on my legs. We worked on exercises in therapy that would strengthen my arms enough to be strong enough to support myself with a walker when the time came. I could only be in the rehab room for so long each day. In the meantime, I would wheel up and down the hall. Trying to build strength in my arms with every push of the wheel. I was amazed at how much strength I didn't have in my healing arm. The long hallway was straight, but I would have to start on the right side of the hallway, because my left arm was so weak, it couldn't push as hard as the right. So I would slowly veer to the left with every push. By the end of the hallway, I was hugging the left side. Day after day it would get a little stronger and stronger. The stronger it got, the straighter I got. It was exhilarating.

I also took it upon myself to try to meet people. One thing I realized is that I was pretty much the youngest patient in the building that I knew of. I think there was one closer to my age, but he was in pretty bad shape and was rarely able to come out of his room. When I was mobile, I felt so bad for him. I felt like I knew what he was going through. Every time I wheeled past his room, I said a little prayer for healing. I could imagine the state of mind he may be in. On the other hand, needless to say, the elderly population was flourishing! I took it upon myself to go eat with them. I like to think they enjoyed it. I'd wheel up to a table and just talk with them. I made a lot of friends that I would have never imagined I'd make. So, I lied about that one time being the last time I'd cry in rehab out of sadness. You know most of these patient's healthcare plans would only allow for them to be in the wing for around twenty-one days. I didn't know that! Some would be in there for even shorter periods of time. I didn't realize a stay as long as mine was quite uncommon. That realization hurt. I'd get attached to them. I remember a gentleman who had early stage dementia. It was sad because there were times where we would be talking and I would turn into his grandson. Then two sentences later, we'd be back to "us" again. But in our basic conversations, we had some of the most profound, spiritual conversations. I truly think we were a blessing to each other. He was the first person I had to say goodbye to when he left the facility. You know by now I'm a softy. I stayed really strong until I got back into the door of my room. I think I spent the next day in hiding. I didn't want to get close to anyone else… but I felt like there were a few that I could try to lift their spirits. At least give them someone to talk to. So I gave it a day and kept pressing on. One by one they would "graduate," and leave. And time after time I would wheel back into my room and let it all out. But it was much needed on both parts. Looking back on it now, I realize that maybe I wasn't helping them so much as they were actually giving ME joy. God was using them to pass His Blessings on to me, lifting my spirits and showing me that I could be a servant again.

As days would pass, I would get stronger and stronger. I was drinking as much milk and protein powder as I could get down in order to get stronger and attempt to build muscle. I finally had my check up for my weight bearing status. I went in to the appointment and honestly, I still had some healing to do. There were a few fragile places on my bones that he just flat out said he didn't know of they'd heal. But he did say that sometimes you just have to stimulate them to get the bone growth active again. So, he released me to be weight bearing that day. I was elated! Also, a little nervous because I realized my legs were still broken, but I was about to attempt to stand on them anyway. I don't know if my therapists got a phone call or what, but they were pretty much waiting for me to get back from that appointment and as soon as I came in the door, they were like, "Let's get you standing!" I'll be honest, I was scared. I didn't realize it would happen that fast. I thought there would be a little bit of transition time there and ease on to them but, nope, apparently the best way is to just try to stand up. So they took me to the therapy room with about five other people, strapped a thing around my waste and gave me instructions. I had a severe case of drop foot. My foot on my bad leg was stuck pointing straight down towards the floor. They say it's normal. It was stiff. I honestly thought it would break if I put weight on it...but regardless, it took a few tries, and a mountain of energy, but they got me on my feet for the first time in months. It was hard. It felt like thousands of straight needles sticking into my legs and feet at the same time. It hurt, but in all of that, it was still easier than I thought it would be to put weight on them. It took a lot of energy. I think I was only able to stand for less than five seconds. But that was enough. The process had begun. I went back to my room and I was so exhausted from standing for less than five seconds, I remember feeling like I had run a whole mile. I fell asleep almost immediately.

From that point on I would take any opportunity to get on a bike, weight machine, or anything else I was allowed to do to gain strength in my legs. I was finally able to work something other than my arms. Every time I stood up, I could go longer and longer. It will surprise anyone how fast that stuff will come back to you. The strength seemed to triple every day. It was amazing! It wasn't long until I could stand up with a walker on my own. Soon after that, they told me it was time to take a step. They wanted to see how far I could go. I felt pretty good, but you just never know. I scrounged up enough energy to stand again, with therapists all around me, I took the sweetest step in my memory. There was a time where we didn't even know if this would be possible. They told me to go as far as I could go. I took the first step and it didn't seem too bad, so I took another, and another, and before long, I had walked over ten feet. I could have gone further, but I didn't have the energy built up yet. The next day I went a little further. Then the next day I walked out of the room. Then I would find spots and try to make it to them each day down the hall. Before long, that same hallway that I veered so far left on in a wheelchair, was now my walking track. It was just a matter of building up enough strength at this point. If I remember right, I had to be able to walk a hundred and twenty feet without sitting down for a rest in order to go home. I'm pretty sure I made it past that point. From there Tandi took me out to learn to get in a vehicle on my own. I had to step up on a curb. Normal, everyday things and encounters that I may run in to. I could see a light at the end of the tunnel. From the day that I stood up for the first time, until the day that I walked out of that place, was less than one month. It is truly amazing what God can do!

Meg had already moved back to Northwest Arkansas with the boys. She had to start teaching again. So I was itching to get home. On the day I graduated from the rehab facility, she came back with my whole family. My Dad, Mom, brothers, friends, and even nurses from UAMS showed up to watch me walk out of there. I was truly blessed. My brothers drove me home and we stopped and ate BBQ! I remember pulling up at home and Dax waiting for me in the driveway. It was so special. It was good to be home!

There were many people at that rehab facility who made a huge impact on my life. I can't begin to tell you how much they are appreciated. I made lifelong friends there and there were days where just simple conversations in the therapy room, lobby, or during wound care treatments, would brighten my day and give me hope. I would have never been able to make it without you all.

Being home was great, but it also had its learning experiences. I had to adjust to a lot of things. I was learning to walk all over again…but I still had a long way to go. I was still in a wheelchair for the majority of the time for the first little while. I would get up and use a walker to the living room, then wheel around the rest of the house. I was also going to therapy sessions to continue strength training. I lost a lot of range of motion in my left ankle. I did exercises to try to get as much of that back as I could. I still don't have a ton of that back. Actually, I'd say I lost eighty-five percent of my range in that ankle. I have a tremendous amount of bone spurs in that joint. It's basically bone on bone and that's about the best they could do for it. It's a daily source of pain but I get by.

One of the biggest setbacks I had to deal with when I got home was overcoming the addiction to pain medication. I was on a bunch of stuff. I don't know how anyone would have made it without it, but there's a time where enough is enough, and you have to find a way to get past it and move on. I was on strong pain medication for that whole time and I had enough to last me around a month when I got home. By the time I got home, I was on eighty milligrams, yes that's e-i-g-h-t-y, of Oxycontin. It was a forty-milligram controlled release tablet that I took twice a day. I wasn't even getting "high." I just knew I didn't hurt. I mean, it was in my system…I was just oblivious to the effects it would have on me. I had taken pain medicine before, obviously not to this magnitude, but my body had never actually been addicted to the medicine. I had made the decision that when I ran out of this bottle, I would just let it go and that'd be the end of it. I figured by then I wouldn't be hurting that bad. So, eventually my supply ran out. It took about thirty days after I got home. One day went by and I was fine. The second day, I felt a little ill in my stomach. The third day, I was dying. I was sweating, coughing, and dry heaving. It felt like someone took a knife and stabbed me in the stomach and when they got done, hit me in the gut with a sledge hammer. I vividly remember that feeling. I couldn't think straight. I was shaking all over. I felt like I had fever without the fever. It was one of the worst feelings I had experienced. What's crazy is that I had no idea what was happening. It never dawned on me. Towards the afternoon on day three, Vaden and Kathleen came over. I knew they were in our living room, but I had myself locked in the bedroom because I couldn't walk out. I just kept coughing and dry heaving. It had to be miserable for them to listen to. I finally mustered up enough to come out and attempt to visit. It was bad. I just looked at Vaden and I said, "Man, I have no idea what's wrong with me."

"When was the last time you took your pain medicine?"

"Three days…"

"We need to get you to a doctor!"

It all made sense now. So, I grabbed my empty pill bottle and went straight to the doctor's office. I have a great primary care physician here in Northwest Arkansas. He is in Bentonville and I drove straight there to try to get in. I was able to see him and I remember just being hunched over in his office when the nurse came in. She asked what the issue was and I gave her the bottle and said, "I'm out of these." She looked at the bottle and immediately said, "Oh my goodness, who gave you these! This is like speed!"

"Like speed huh? That explains a lot."

"We've got to get this under control. We'll take care of it."

So finally, my doctor came in. I love this guy. He's been a good friend over the years and I feel like he just gets me. That's always a positive to have in your primary care physician. I asked him why I was feeling the way I was and he promptly told me that my body was in withdrawals. I asked him how long it would last. He said it could be anywhere from a few days to a few weeks. I said, "No, I can't do that. I just can't. I need help now."

"I can help you. There's an easy way, and a hard way. The hard way is waiting it out. You could be done soon and that's it. OR, I can ween you off them and it will go much easier."

"The ween thing…let's do that."

So, he wrote me a prescription for a smaller dose. He cut the dose in half and said to take them for thirty days and then come back and see him. So, that's what I did. I went to my pharmacy and gave them the prescription. I had to show a hundred and eleven forms of identification, give eight fingerprints, and a blood and urine sample, but I got them filled… barely. I got in the truck at the pharmacy and took one of the pills. My doctor told me to take one as soon as possible. There's about a ten minute drive from my pharmacy to home. By the time I made it home, put some comfortable clothes on, and laid down in bed, I was already feeling better. Another twenty minutes, and I had zero withdrawal symptoms. I knew the symptoms themselves were bad. But, I didn't fully grasp the scope of the problem until I realized how fast my body adjusted to getting what it wanted. That scared me more than anything. I laid in bed and cried because I couldn't believe I was addicted to pain medicine. I don't really know why I was so shocked. I mean, who wouldn't be addicted to pain medicine at this point? There's just times where you think you're immune to such things and when it finally hits you, you realize how serious that issue is in a lot of people's lives. I knew I had to make a decision right now to make sure I did what I was supposed to do to rid myself of the stress of being dependent on these things. Right now I had a doctor that was more than willing to help. I needed to take advantage of that. One day he's going to stop prescribing these for me and if I don't do what I'm supposed to do, my body will still crave them. I know exactly what that addiction feels like and I don't want to EVER be in a situation where I'm so desperate to stop it, that I feel the need to do something illegal to fix it. You may think that assessment is extreme, but I know what it feels like when your body wants it and you don't have it. I can't imagine being in a situation where I don't have a way out of it. It really is no wonder why so many people struggle with this. If you're having a problem, there are many avenues for pain management other than this. I know there are instances where you just need something and I completely understand that. But, your body starts needing more and more of them to react to that pain just like any other drug you may encounter. Whether you're needing the drug for pain, or just simply getting the great feeling from them, eventually your body will need more to accomplish the goal you're seeking from them. There is a point where that physician will stop supplying that to you. You don't even want to be in a position where you have to do something irrational to ease your symptoms. "Well, you're obviously stronger than I am, there's no way I can do that!' No, I'm not. I'm not any stronger than you. There just comes a time where you have to wake up and make a conscious decision to stop it. Yes it hurts, yes there is extreme pain, and yes I have chronic kidney stones and I still have to take them at times, but when I'm done, I'm done. If I have to, I'll get Meg to hide them until I need them again. But, my sincere advice is to find a physician who will help you through the process. If that physician can trust you, and you prove that to them, they will help you.

I went back a month later and I really don't know what I was thinking, but I thought maybe we'd be done and I could just stop taking them. I made that comment like, "So, is that it?" That's when he explained to me that it wasn't an overnight fix. I was taking a very large amount of this stuff. He actually couldn't believe that I was sent home with it. But it would take more than a few months. He asked if I felt any withdrawal symptoms during the time I was taking the new dosage and I didn't feel any at all. So, he cut the dosage in half again, told me if I started feeling any signs of withdrawal to call him immediately. I went from forty-milligrams, to twenty-milligrams, to ten. He told me to come back in thirty more days…and I did. We eventually moved on to Percocet. Another shot in my gut. See, I don't know anything about this stuff…what goes in them, what class of drug they are, what active ingredients? I don't have a clue. But what I DO know is Percocet is a pretty hefty drug itself. Every stage of this intervention was another light shed on the issue. I knew I was taking some potent stuff. But when two Percocets is like step four or five in the step down process of these things, it was serious. The good news is these pills could be cut up, or split doses. The previous were all controlled release so I had to take the whole pill. Now I was at my own pace. He wanted to monitor it, so he told me to make a chart. I may have went a little overkill on the chart but that's me! I went and made a spreadsheet and literally had twenty-four time slot squares for each hour of the day. Then every row was a day of the month. When I took a dose, I would draw one circle for each pill. If I split it, I would draw a half-circle. If I cut it into quarters, I would draw a line. My doctor said it was up to me how I felt but to see if I could tolerate stretching a dose an extra hour here and there, but to never let myself get too far into symptoms. Eventually, if I did my chart right, my dosing marks would start to make a pattern and taper to the right as they moved down the chart and eventually they would taper away. So, at first, I'd have two full circles every four hours. After a few days, I decided to try waiting an extra hour. So I was at two full circles for five hours now. That went really well for day one of that experiment, so on day two, I tried to wait a full six hours. It went without a hitch. I did that for a day or so then I thought, I may be able to get away with cutting one in half. So, my doses were now a full circle and a half every six hours. I could feel a few symptoms when I made this adjustment, but it wasn't anything I couldn't handle. I kept tapering, and tapering, and within another three weeks, my chart was down to a single line every eight hours. I was able to cut those into quarters and take a small sliver of that pill...and eventually I just stopped taking them and was able to discard the rest of them. Now, I realize I could have probably just stopped taking them by that point. I probably wouldn't have felt much. But part of the process here for me was knowing I had a system, and I was able to finish it until the end. I was also probably more addicted to watching the pattern my marks made of those dosing records go down that chart too, Ha! On my last check-up with him, I gave him my chart and he kept it for my file. He was excited and so was I. I'll say it again, he has helped me more than he will ever realize over the years. My hope is that one day he will read this and realize that he's made an impact on my life in far greater ways than he probably even realizes. He's an integral part of my recovery, and it means the world to me. Thank you, Dr. Bicak.

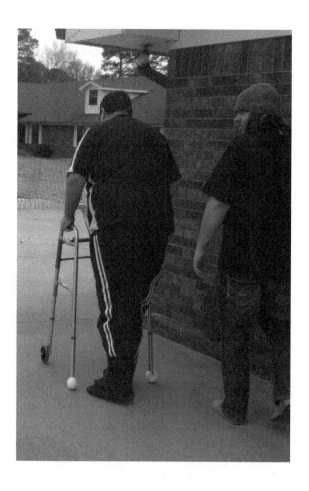

# 11

# WHAT I'VE LEARNED

There is zero doubt in my mind that it was God's will for me to go through this trial. I knew I would have a story to share and I knew that God would need it to be shared. So there's a few reasons you could be reading this book. For starters, you know me personally, you're a friend, a member of our church, and for that I say thank you. Maybe you randomly stumbled on this book and thought it may be an inspirational read. I hope it has lived up to your expectations so far. Then there are those of you who need this story. You're here searching for help in any way you can get it. Maybe you need answers, you need a story, and the specific details in this one to confirm that there's something out there that's higher than us...that loves us unconditionally. I'm no biblical scholar, I'll be the first to let you know that. But I can share with you what I've learned and the things that I know will get you to a point in your life where you can live in peace, knowing there's someone out there that cares for you...no matter who you are, what choices you've made, how bad you think you are, or have been. I get it, sometimes we just need a little reassurance. Sometimes we get knocked off track. Sometimes the events in our life have caused us to lose faith in what we have. Discouragement. It's the enemy's biggest weapon. I've been there.

There are so many places I can start here. One very effective thing about being able to tell your own story, is that you are directly able to relate the feelings you've had and experienced to someone else. In the end, the person you share them with can know that you're not just making it up, but you've actually lived through it. Through my experience, I think the best place to get the ball rolling is to let you know that you are never alone. There's nothing you can ever do to escape God's love, so stop beating yourself up thinking you're worthless. No matter how worthless you think you are, God always has someone out there looking up to you. It's your decision to make the right choice that whatever that person sees in you is godly, and good. If you fall into the pit of self-defeat, you're only falling into the trap of the enemy, and handcuffing whatever the Holy Spirit is striving to do in your life. Sometimes God puts you in situations to keep you there until you figure out His purpose for you. Listen here, this is very important, if you haven't heard anything yet, hear this… get a highlighter, circle it, whatever you have to do…

Not everything that happens in your past defines you, but God will use everything in your past to define Himself, through you.

Sometimes we just go through stuff. You want to know why? I have absolutely no idea. But I know God does. Sometimes it's by our own choice. Our own freedom. Sometimes things are allowed to happen. Sometimes we just need to wake up. But what I can tell you is God doesn't make mistakes. You know that. So the only thing we are left to do is trust that whatever He brings, or allows to come our way, is actually PERFECT in His eyes. I know that sounds absolutely crazy, but it's true. And if he brings it to us, it may not be fun, but we will be equipped with every tool to survive what's here upon us. You know, sometimes you just have to lay on your behind in a hospital bed, to truly and fully grasp what God has planned for your life. It really is that simple. When you're a child of God, and going through these trials, you're going to get attacked left and right. The enemy knows God. He knows God has a plan and he'll do whatever he can to knock you off task. He knows what he's up against, Y'all. Listen, James 2:19 says:

"You say you have faith, for you believe that there is one God. Good for you! Even the demons believe this, and they tremble in terror!"

Knock! Knock! Hello?!? Even your enemy trembles in terror at the power of the God you serve. Why on Earth do we ever question anything that God has in store for us? That alone should give you the courage you need! Don't let your guard down! If you find yourself in the midst of a trial in your life, keep these things in mind, and then pray for clarity in your life so that you can see what God has planned for you.

I believe in a Creator. I believe He loves us and will do anything for his Children, and now to move further you have to ask yourself if you are one of His children. You may not have peace at all. Your life may be packed full of things that shouldn't be there. God's Word calls it sin. I'm not preaching at you. I need you to know that I'm a broken man. I struggle with things every day. For me to sit here and tell you that you're wrong, in my eyes, would be hypocritical. What I can tell you is what God's Words says and I'm just as responsible for following that as you are. I'm not a hero, I'm not a person to hold high on some pedestal, I'm a broken man, I've made huge mistakes, and I had a few things go wrong in life and I let them get the best of me. People have said "You're an inspiration!" I appreciate that, but without God I am nothing. Listen, I used to put my faith in man. I told you that earlier. A great friend of mine once told me "Anyone who is less than God, will fail you at some point in your life." I will never forget that. So I need to tell you, if you're reading this and God uses my story to help you, then I am so happy and I thank the Lord that He used me. But one day, if we know each other long enough, I will fail you. It is up to you to take the information you gain and use it to further God's Kingdom. So you know that I have struggled with things in my life. I still have to fight things off daily like every single Christian does in their own lives. If they say they don't, they need to do a deep reevaluation of their lives. But again, if your life is packed full of things that shouldn't be there, and you're looking for help and clarity, then my advice to you is to truly search God's Word. It doesn't matter what you think, what you feel, what political affiliation you may have… God's Word is still His Word. You can't change it to fit your personal beliefs. You can't change it to make you feel better for the day. You can't change it to justify anything you've ever done, thought about doing, or will do in the future. God's Word is Forever His Word. My dad once told me, "Hutch, there comes a time in your life where you have to make a choice to believe in God. Do you believe in Him or not? If so, then you have to decide to believe in Him and believe He is who He says He is and He will do what He says He'll do. There's no middle ground." That's where we sit right now. If you're looking for answers, you either believe or you don't, it's that simple. You can walk away right now, and continue on with your life the way it has been, or you can make a choice today, at this moment, to put every ounce of Faith in God, believe, turn away from those things that shouldn't be there, and accept what comes your way. In Matthew 11:28, Jesus says"

"Come to me, all of you who are weary and carry heavy burdens, and I will give you rest."

Y'all, our Creator wants to forgive you! Why do we battle that? The only thing that can quit on us… is us, God's love never quits!

So the first thing we have to do in our healing process is determine if we truly believe in God, and have we personally, without any shame, doubt, or reserve, chosen to follow Him? That's a question you must ask yourself right now. None of this other stuff even matters until that's determined. I can tell you, you're going to be alone if you don't. Why would anyone want to go through this stuff alone? But it has to be your decision. Maybe you're reading this and you're thinking "Well I've already done this, I know where I'm headed and I truly believe!" Well, your time is coming in a few moments, but before I go any further, I just want to make sure everyone is on the same page here.

Y'all, this is what I believe. I believe everyone is born with a sinful nature, and we all do bad things. We all sin. Because of that, we fall short of God's Glory (Romans 3:23.) And Romans 3:10 says:

"No one is righteous, not even one."

Not one person is good, and the punishment for our lifestyles is death. Plain and simple. But in the midst of all of this, God offers us the gift of eternal life (Romans 6:23.) The only way the price of our sin could be paid, was for an innocent, sinless man to suffer in our place. God demonstrated His endless love for you, by allowing His Son to die for you (Romans 5:8.) Look here, Jesus died for you, knowing who you were, what you would do, say, every mocking word, every single evil thing you would do… and He did it anyway, and He wasn't scared of anything you may one day bring Him. There is no greater act of Love that I can imagine.

So knowing all of that, you have an opportunity to turn away from those things, start fresh, and live serving a wonderful Creator that loves you unconditionally. All you have to bring to the table is yourself. Romans 10: 9-13 says:

"…that if you confess with your mouth Jesus as Lord, and believe in your heart that God raised Him from the dead, you will be saved; for with the heart a person believes, resulting in righteousness, and with the mouth he confesses, resulting in salvation. For the Scripture says whoever believes in Him will not be disappointed. For there is no distinction between Jew and Greek; for the same Lord is Lord of all, abounding in riches for all who call on Him; for whoever will call upon the Lord will be saved."

With that, I ask you to take a moment and reflect on your life. Maybe you've never fully committed to believing. As the Scripture says, "You will not be disappointed." I encourage you to take a moment, pray, and fully commit to God right now. There is no single prayer that will get you into Heaven. You may say, "I appreciate this, but I do great things in my church all the time and I do good things for people I don't even know." There's no good deed that will get you in the proper relationship with Christ. There's not enough you can do on your own to work enough to get you there. Ephesians 2: 8-9 says:

"For by grace you have been saved through FAITH; and that not of yourselves, it is the GIFT of GOD; not as a result of works, so that no one may boast."

God doesn't want you to work like that FOR it. He wants you to have true Faith and Believe…and he will give it to you. It's your decision. As I said before, I can't make you do it and nothing else after this will matter if this decision isn't made now. But if you're going to be a child of God, and claim that you know Him, and you want to know, that you know, that you know, that when you go from this Earth, that you will be in His presence, then in my belief, according to Scripture I believe in, this is the decision that is required to inherit His kingdom. Take a moment now, pray, it doesn't matter how good you are at it, or even if you've never done it before. It doesn't matter how old or young you are. It doesn't matter what church you go to, what denomination, if any, what matters is that you've personally made a commitment to the one that created you…to truly believe in Him, follow his lead, and never look back. "I'm not good enough, I don't even go to church!" If you open your heart and are willing to accept Him, He gives you the right to become a child of God (John 1:12.) Pray now and let God know you believe in Him, let Him know that you believe that He sent His Son to die and take the place of your sins and that He rose again for you. Let Him know that you're sorry and truly ask for the forgiveness that He offers, and that you repent and commit to turn away from the things that distract you and the sins in your life. If you do these things, I truly believe you will be washed and made new. It's very possible that God put me through all of these things in my life for YOU to be sitting at this very moment, reading this, and making this decision. If that's the case, I would do it all over again… I truly would. You're reading this now for a reason. Don't discredit that. If you're willing, take that time now. Accept His forgiveness and promise of eternal life.

If you just took the time to make that commitment, Congratulations! You just took the most important step in your walk with Christ. It gets me teary eyed knowing that one day we will celebrate this decision together in Glory! You ARE good enough. You're a new creature. 2 Corinthians 5:17 says:

"Therefore if anyone is in Christ, he is a new creature; the old things passed away; behold, new things have come!"

Take a deep breath and know that everything in your life now belongs to God and He promises to see it through! You're going to be fought…but rest assured you will have every tool necessary to defeat everything that comes your way. The Holy Spirit now lives in you. When you veer off path, you will be reminded which way to go. You still have a choice, but the Spirit will guide you the right way and convict you when you've done wrong. If that happens, don't beat yourself up, just keep turning and running towards what God has planned. One of the biggest things to remember is there are a lot of people making their life long spiritual decisions and choices based on what they see you do and hear you say. Keep that in mind. You may be the single person that God wants to show Himself through in someone else's life. Don't mess that up. Stay focused and help others reach the prize that you have now found. Remember, God may be using the trial you're going through right now, to be the single story that helps someone do exactly what you just did. Let God use you.

I encourage you to go and find a great study book, get yourself engulfed in the Word. You're not going to know everything right now. You are beginning your journey. Surround yourself with great people. Keep digging. No matter how hard it gets, keep on keeping on. You can do it!

Now that everyone is on the same page, maybe you are in the shoes I was in. Maybe you made a commitment long ago and events in your life started dragging you down over time. Maybe someone has come in to your life and tried to alter your way of thinking. You know what's there, you know where your heart is, but you've allowed someone to open the door of doubt. You want to be accepted by them. You want them to love you…but you feel like they may not because of your religious views. I hear you. That's hard. Deuteronomy 31:8 says:

"The Lord is the one who goes ahead of you; He will be with you. He will not fail you or forsake you. Do not fear or be dismayed."

The Lord will never forsake you. So if you turn on Him, that's your decision. But I can tell you, if you are truly a child of His, He WILL get you back on path. You're still here for a reason. He will put you in a position, believe me, to carry out what He has planned for you! Hey, you may be the only hope those around you have. I promise the enemy isn't working on them like he is you. If he takes you out, he knows he has them too.

Stay strong and fight, knowing that God is on your side. In this world today there are going to be plenty of people that will make you doubt everything. Some of them, that's their intention. For whatever reason they may have, you can't be led astray. I think some of the most encouraging words here come from John Chapter 16 which say:

"I've told you these things to prepare you for rough times ahead. They are going to throw you out of the meeting places. There will even come a time when anyone who kills you will think he's doing God a favor. They will do these things because they never really understood the Father. I've told you these things so that when the time comes and they start in on you, you'll be well-warned and ready for them. But now I am on my way to the One who sent me. Not one of you has asked, 'Where are you going? Instead, the longer I've talked, the sadder you've become. So let me say it again, this truth: It's better for you that I leave. If I don't leave, the Friend won't come. But if I go, I'll send him to you. "When he comes, he'll expose the error of the godless world's view of sin, righteousness, and judgment: He'll show them that their refusal to believe in me is their basic sin; that righteousness comes from above, where I am with the Father, out of their sight and control; that judgment takes place as the ruler of this godless world is brought to trial and convicted. "I still have many things to tell you, but you can't handle them now. But when the Friend comes, the Spirit of the Truth, he will take you by the hand and guide you into all the truth there is. He won't draw attention to himself, but will make sense out of what is about to happen and, indeed, out of all that I have done and said. He will honor me; he will take from me and deliver it to you. Everything the Father has is also mine. That is why I've said, 'He takes from me and delivers to you.'

"In a day or so you're not going to see me, but then in another day or so you will see me." That stirred up a hornet's nest of questions among the disciples: "What's he talking about: 'In a day or so you're not going to see me, but then in another day or so you will see me'? And, 'Because I'm on my way to the Father'? What is this 'day or so'? We don't know what he's talking about." Jesus knew they were dying to ask him what he meant, so he said, "Are you trying to figure out among yourselves what I meant when I said, 'In a day or so you're not going to see me, but then in another day or so you will see me'? Then fix this firmly in your minds: You're going to be in deep mourning while the godless world throws a party. You'll be sad, very sad, but your sadness will develop into gladness. "When a woman gives birth, she has a hard time, there's no getting around it. But when the baby is born, there is joy in the birth. This new life in the world wipes out memory of the pain. The sadness you have right now is similar to that pain, but the coming joy is also similar. When I see you again, you'll be full of joy, and it will be a joy no one can rob from you. You'll no longer be so full of questions. Ask in my name, according to my will, and he'll most certainly give it to you. Your joy will be a river overflowing its banks! "I've used figures of speech in telling you these things. Soon I'll drop the figures and tell you about the Father in plain language. Then you can make your requests directly to him in relation to this life I've revealed to you. I won't continue making requests of the Father on your behalf. I won't need to. Because you've gone out on a limb, committed yourselves to love and trust in me, believing I came directly from the Father, the Father loves you directly. First, I left the Father and arrived in the world; now I leave the world and travel to the Father." His disciples said, "Finally! You're giving it to us straight, in plain talk - no more figures of speech.

Now we know that you know everything - it all comes together in you. You won't have to put up with our questions anymore. We're convinced you came from God." Jesus answered them, "Do you finally believe? In fact, you're about to make a run for it - saving your own skins and abandoning me. But I'm not abandoned. The Father is with me. I've told you all this so that trusting me, you will be unshakable and assured, deeply at peace. In this godless world you will continue to experience difficulties. But take heart! I've conquered the world."

He has already conquered the world! There's no need to question anything. As I said before, there comes a time in life where you have to make a choice. You either believe or you don't. If you do, you have to believe everything and go through your life knowing it's truth. If others abandon you, that may be what God has planned. Those people also have a decision to make. If they wait or fail to make that decision, that's their choice. It will be hard to let them go. But you have to leave it in God's hands. Pray for them. Encourage them. Be an example. If they decided to walk away, just know it's by their choice. You have a huge responsibility to fulfil God's purpose for your life. There are so many people willing to accept what He has for them. Don't let these distractions hinder you from doing that. You never know, as much as you want it to be, God may actually have someone else in His plans to restore your loved ones. It may not be you.

If you've let bitterness take over your life...let it go. I know it sounds easier said than done. But again, you have a responsibility to fulfil a greater purpose. There's simply no room for bitterness. No matter where you go to church, remember what we talked about before, no one person is righteous. Anyone less than God will fail you. Church staff, leaders, none of them are perfect. They all struggle with the same sins that you struggle with. The enemy knows they're leaders. He hits them even harder. He knows that if they fall, a lot of people will lose faith in church as it sits. Don't fall victim to that. If a leader in your life finds themselves in trouble, be the first to offer help and prayer, and be the one that God used to guide them back to serving His greater purpose. No one, and I mean no one, is out of the realm of temptation and discouragement. Keep that in mind. I can't tell you how many people I've encountered that were the first people to point out someone's sin, yet years later, were exposed to have fallen victim to the same sin. Don't give the enemy the opportunity either way. Don't be that person in the back of the church that talks and spreads the negativity. Your church will not continue to be effective until everyone is spiritually healed and back on track. The spreading of that negativity, even in your facial expressions, your drive to attend and be involved, and how you display your attitude over the situation will directly affect your spirit, the churches spirit, and can possibly be the single reason someone isn't reached. The enemy will use a tragic situation, and make you, the self-righteous "believer," the sole person responsible for the damage. Don't be that person. Don't let your guard down. If you find yourself with those feelings, go find a room at your church, close the door, and spend time praying for your church and its leaders. If all else fails, find a room and pray. It's much better to hide yourself than let the enemy use you to divide. That just doesn't go with church issues, but with life in general. Don't be the negative weight that your friends and family constantly have to carry around. I've been that person before. It's not fun. You're not a victim. You're a child of God. As soon as you realize that, and stop letting the enemy rob you of your Joy, you're going to be a more productive member of society, your family, and most of all, God's purpose. Get back on the horse and pony up, friend!

Finally, if the enemy is using your sin, past and present, to keep you down…stop it. You're a child of God. Yes, there are times you're going to stumble. If you do, keep pushing on. Everything has been washed away. You can't let yourself get to a point of such despair that you are spiritually paralyzed. I was so afraid of being labeled a hypocrite. Everything I struggled with would hit me in the face every time I was asked to do anything that involved God. It took my confidence away. It took my purpose. I was so handcuffed by the guilt of sin, that I didn't feel worthy to do God's work. Those very feelings left me in a deep state of depression. That depression led to me being the guy in the back of the church. The one that couldn't trust anyone. I wanted to know what sins they were hiding while they were preaching or on stage. That's what I dealt with. I didn't listen. I didn't want to listen. In my head I thought "there's no way this person is that happy, righteous, and godly." Bitterness was an understatement. Every door you open for the enemy leads to another, and another, and another. Before long, any drive you had to fulfil God's purpose has left you. You've successfully become irrelevant…. And I'm here to tell you, if God still has you breathing on this Earth, He still has a plan for your life. You better find it, or He may put you in a position where you have no other choice but to find it. Your life is never a waste. You can always be restored. You just have to let yourself be restored. Pick up the pieces. Do whatever it takes to put those pieces together. Get yourself back on track.

# 12

# HOW IT REALLY ENDS

In October of 2015, almost two years after my accident, I was down visiting my family and cooking BBQ for an event in Smackover. I was about to head back to Northwest Arkansas. We got back from church and my dad said "Hey let's go ride through the deer woods before you go home, ok?" I never turned down an opportunity to go riding with him. We rolled through the first stretch of the deer lease and he talked about how happy he was to be there and how pretty it was. After the first curve they had clear cut a few acres of timber and honestly, it was devastating. We had ridden through that stretch of woods quite a few times. Now it was flattened. He was legitimately sad and for good reason. I remember telling him that I had come through that stretch a few weeks earlier and took a video of my drive to capture the woods one more time before they cut them and he was very happy to hear that.

We made our way through along the same path that we always took. The roads wind and turn, it would be easy for the novice to get lost, but we could drive them with our eyes closed.

A couple of miles in the woods we were getting close to the spot of my accident. I had not yet even stepped foot on the plot of land where that happened. As we got closer, I said...

"Dad, let's stop here and go out there…I think I'm ready."

"Why do you want to go out there? You don't want to go out there."

"I think I'm ok with it, Dad. Let's do it!"

"Son, you're about to go through some things…I feel like you're about to go through some things and you're going to have a lot on you. You don't need the stress of reliving that right now."

I was puzzled. I kind of looked at him like "Bro, are you crazy?" I even joked with him and called him Nostradamus.

"What are you talking about? What are you, Nostradamus?"

He actually chuckled, grinned, then started tearing up and said,

"Son, if something happens to me, I need you and your brothers to do a few things…"

"What things? Dad, what are you talking about? You're scaring me right now. Nothing is going to happen to you. Let's just stop talking about it and keep riding."

"But you need to know this stuff, Son."

"Well, not right now. No way."

Being himself, he told me stuff anyway until I finally talked him into changing the subject. I didn't think much of it. It bothered me, but I seriously didn't feel like there was anything to worry about. He didn't have any terminal illnesses…the subject just came up. What's to worry about, right?

Cliff had called us and we left the woods. Cliff wanted us to meet him for lunch so we drove to El Dorado and had a bite to eat. Dad had to go back into his office. He asked Cliff to take me back to Smackover and drop me off so I could head out of town. I hugged my Dad, told him I loved him, and I vividly remember watching him walk away and get into his truck.

You know, originally, the story was supposed to be over by now. I feel like I've talked about a number of "Events" that happened in my life during this time. There's one person who truly deserves to read this book, and that person won't be able to. It's completely heartbreaking. As I said before, this was supposed to be over. A happy ending to the book and everything would be great. People could hear my story and hopefully God would use it to help someone. God had a different plan.

I was in the final stages of editing this book. Every day I continued to get better and better. It's a long process. As I mentioned earlier, one of my main goals was to be back hunting again by the next season and that I accomplished. Dad and I had been in contact by phone after I left that afternoon and we had finalized a date (Thursday November 12th) to do our work and then hunt on opening day that coming Saturday. It had been three or so weeks since I was last home in Smackover. On November 3rd, my birthday, Dad called me to wish me a Happy Birthday. I loved talking to him. I asked him how he was doing and he said "I feel great. I feel better than I have in a long time." We talked for a while. Mostly about hunting. Dax's birthday was a couple weeks before so he wanted to tell Dax that he had planned on having a big birthday party for all of his grandkids around Thanksgiving and he was so excited. He always wanted to talk to "The Daxter," as he called him. Dax and Kannyn (Cliff's Daughter) also known as "Bang Bang" to my Dad were born exactly eight days apart. I got the phone back and talked to my Dad some more. It was time to hang up and he said "Well Son, I just wanted to wish you a Happy Birthday and let you know I love you." I said "I love you too, Dad…" and we hung up. I felt so good after the call. He sounded so good. I remember thinking, "Man he sounded great today, and he really sounded peaceful."

The next day I tried to call my Dad during the early afternoon. He didn't answer which wasn't too uncommon. I tried to call Dave and Cliff, and they didn't answer, again, not uncommon. So I just waited around and got back to doing some things. A few minutes later, I got a phone call from Cliff and he said "Hey man, you need to come home." He was crying.

"What's wrong? What in the world is wrong?"

"Something happened to Dad, an ambulance took him to the E.R.…he's not responding…you need to come home pretty quick."

My Dad was having trouble breathing. So he called my Uncle Larry to come get him and take him to the doctor. They got about half way there and my Dad told my Uncle that he didn't think he was going to make it there. He couldn't breathe and he was hurting. So my Uncle called an ambulance and had them meet him. My Dad walked to the ambulance, lay down on the stretcher, and went unresponsive.

I hung up the phone. Meg had just come home from school. I sat on the edge of my bed and suddenly everything that I thought mattered over the last few years, what I had been through, it didn't seem to matter anymore. I just remember sitting there, I couldn't breathe, Meg was panicking…she just started packing clothes and suitcases. She didn't even have to ask. She knew it wasn't good. "My God…My God…My God…Please God, No." I just remember saying that over and over. I still couldn't catch my breath. Meg loaded the kids and stuff in the car. It felt like slow motion as I walked from the bedroom to the door…locked the door, and started to the car. Living far away, I had always feared something happening to one of my family and having to make the 5-6 hour drive, not having a clue about what the outcome would be…and here I was living out that fear. I wasn't getting many updates…mainly because there weren't many. I got a call from my aunt and she said that he may have started responding…but she wasn't sure. I knew he was still alive, but that's all I knew. I drove as fast as I could, holding on to any hope that I could muster up.

We arrived at the hospital a few hours later and outside waiting for us was Dave and Wayne. I looked at Dave and naturally asked "How is he?" Dave said "he's not good man."

"So he's not been responding at all?"

"No man, none…it's just a waiting game right now."

So when Dad went unresponsive, it took them another ten or so minutes to get to the hospital. He was without oxygen for approximately fifteen minutes. They worked on him in the E.R. and were able to get a faint heartbeat back. When they did, they immediately took him to surgery to remove the clot from his heart. By the time I made it, he was on a ventilator, and still not responding.

I made my way up to see him. I hated looking at him like that. I may have cried harder in those fifteen minutes than I ever have in my entire life. The man didn't know how to wear socks. Half the time they would hang half off his feet and bunched up. I could see those feet there with those socks sticking out. No one had taken them off yet. I remember reaching up and trying to fix them...I don't know why. There was nothing I could do but be there and pray. We tried talking to him. The nurse said "Just keep talking you never know." So we talked. For four days we prayed, and we talked.

On day four they were able to get him stable enough to do an EEG to test his brain activity. Due to his brain being deprived of oxygen for so long, they didn't know if his body would make it without the ventilator. One of Dad's best friends was his doctor. Usually doctors are pretty stoic...especially this friend. I saw him come out and talk to Cliff...I've never seen him cry, but he was pretty welled up. I knew it wasn't good. As brothers, we prayed, and made the hardest decision we've ever had to make...but we made sure to do it as brothers. Our Dad wouldn't have had it any other way. I remember we went down to try to eat a bite of lunch and got a call that we needed to come back to the ICU waiting room. They brought us into a chapel they had close by. With all of my family present, another doctor had come in. I think it was just too much on Dad's friend. This doctor was a member at the church where Cliff was on staff as worship pastor. He walked in and had his head down. He just kind of looked up, sadly, and uttered the words "Mr. Preston…Mr. Preston has passed." You know, as much as you think you can be ready for something…you're never ready. I will never forget that moment. Complete and total heartbreak. The finality hits you in the face and it was one of the worst feelings in the world. All I could think about was two years ago to this day. November 8th. My accident was on November 8th…and here I was exactly two years later to the day and within the exact hour…I've lost my Dad. All I could do is imagine his face right there when they were loading me up on that ambulance. His tears. His hurt. I felt guilty. Maybe I should have smiled that day? Man, I was a wreck. My brothers were a wreck. Poor Dave was trying his best to be the strong one and we all just walked around trying our best to be strong…but it was the worst fog I think we've ever been in. A few of us went back to be with Dad. Together, Dave, Cliff, Mom, and Myself, had a small private moment with him. I don't want to share too many details of that moment, but one I will. Dave stood and said, "Y'all, we have put a black mark on this day, November 8th, because of Hutch's accident and everything that has happened…but today, from now on, we will be happy on November 8th, because it's the day our Daddy went to be with our Lord." That was encouragement we needed. Up until that moment, it was almost as if the accident had defined me. I have friends down in the Gulf and they talk about Hurricane Katrina and refer to time as "Before the storm," or "After the storm," and for a time, that's where I was. But on this day, it wasn't important. I had a story, yes. But the accident, from this day forward, would not define who I was.

We buried Dad on November 12th…the day he and I

had scheduled to get ready for deer season. In all of the fog, I got to thinking about that old hunting truck Dad drove. I actually drive it now. It's still scarred with dents and scratches. Those are mainly from the day of my accident. Not long ago someone suggested that I try to remove some of the larger dents. I simply replied "No Way! That's character." Only today I truly realize what it is and what that character actually means. Those dents and scratches show me the love of my father. As I said earlier, when he heard the commotion, he tried to drive straight to me... through trees, brush, over stumps, hitting tree trunks risking his own life to get to his child as fast as he could. He didn't care about the damage of the truck, his love and determination to save his son trumped all of that. So when I look at my old beat up truck, I remember the unwavering love of my father. I will never forget it.

You know, I hated leaving home. When deer season came and went, Dad and I looked forward to it so much, that when it was over, we literally cried. I remember once before my accident I had used all of the tags I had for deer harvesting and I was fortunate enough to use them up in only a few days. He sent me a text after I shot a deer and said "Did you get it? Sounded like you got it?"

"Yep! I got it!"

"Great! I'm gonna hunt some more so why don't you come over and sit with me."

Being that I had no tags left, I thought it'd be fun to go sit with him again. So I did. I climbed up that stand with him and it was fun. It was a little sad too because I knew that was it for my hunting that season and he did too. I had to sit a little behind him in that deer stand and I glanced at him and noticed a tear rolling down his cheek. I knew what he was crying for. I said "Are you crying?" He chuckled and then I started tearing up. That's just who we are. When each season was over before going home I'd go sit on the foot of his bed and he'd lay there and we'd talk about the week. Mostly crying because it was over. Honestly, we both feared each season could be our last together. He usually held up pretty strong until I kind of busted him once. I had left and got about ten miles down the road and had to come back. I walked back in to grab something and I went to tell him bye again, and he was a mess. Face red, tears everywhere…a snotty mess. "You ok?"

"Yeah Mutch I'm fine." (He called me Mutch)

"Well ok you're scaring me!"

"I'm ok, buddy. Love you. Be careful."

"Love you too."

Stacey followed me out of the house. I said "What in the world is going on with him?"

"Oh he's ok. He does this every time you leave."

"Wait, what?!? Seriously?!"

"Yes but he's ok. He'll be ok."

It broke my heart, Y'all. So I went in and talked with him about it. We got a good cry out. So from then on, we just cried before I left, Ha! The cat was out of the bag. I missed being home with him. I'm so glad I got that last deer season with him…the one fresh back from my accident. I couldn't have

asked for a better one. I remember when I left from that week,
I went to sit on his bed…ready to cry it out. I know it seems
like an unmanly thing to do. You know, sit and hunt animals all
week then cry because it's over. That's just who we are, Ha!
But I noticed he wasn't crying. "You're not crying!"

"And you better stop!" He said. "We've been through too much
to get emotional like this. This year, let's be thankful we had a
good season and enjoy the time we have. We'll start today on
preparing for next year. No more tears!"

"That sounds like a great plan, Dad!"

It's kind of crazy how that was actually the last one…then again,
it's almost poetic. But I wouldn't have traded how it ended for
the world.

 I've learned so much from the death of my father. I had
literally feared the day, you know? If you ever had the pleasure
of meeting him, you know he had the perfect words to say
when you needed them most. It seemed every question you
ever had he could answer it and make you feel so much better
in a matter of minutes. He never sugar coated things, but even
in his brutal truth, he had a way of relaying the message to you
in a way that made you feel special and that you could
accomplish anything. He left us with valuable life lessons. One
of which being to treat other people with love at all times. He
would always say "Son always be thoughtful and loving when
you talk to people. You never know what they're going through
and what they have to go home to. Whatever you say to them
could be the encouragement they needed, or the negativity that
pushes them over the edge." He also taught us to say "I love
you." Whenever we leave each other; our brothers, mom, dad,

we say I love you. When the conversation or visit ends, it's "I love you." He would always say "You never know when the last time you talk to your brothers or dad and mom will be…Always tell them you love them." That's what we do. I talked with Dave, Cliff, and Wayne, and we all four know beyond any shadow of doubt that our last words we each heard and spoke to our father were "I love you."

My Dad taught us how to love the Lord. His mission in life was to spread the gospel. His race is now finished. While talking with my brothers, we have all realized just how special our Dad was. We knew he meant a lot to many people, but we never realized the magnitude of the amount of lives God used him to touch. We are completely overwhelmed and overjoyed by the amount of thankfulness for my father's life. As we discussed our fears of being without our Dad, we quickly came to the conclusion that our Dad was the enemy's biggest threat. God used him so much to touch so many lives. Our request, and our goal for ourselves is to mourn, but to move on. Carry on the legacy he left. If we all give up because he is gone, then the enemy wins. We are all that's left of a great legacy. We will pick up his torch and carry on. The enemy thinks he won, but people, we have news for him, God wins! God used my dad David Preston in mighty ways. He has built an army of supporters and warriors.

Finally, as this all comes to an end…as much as I hated losing my Dad, through his death, I'm reminded of so much God showed me, through him. I know he always prayed for God to at least let him live long enough to know his boys were going to be ok. I truly feel like God honored that. I actually stayed and hunted after his funeral…for him. On that Saturday,

Dave harvested the biggest deer any of us have ever taken in our lives. I don't think that was by chance. Most of the season I just kind of sat and stared and cried a lot. When that week was over…I went to sit at the foot of my Dad's bed and he wasn't there. I hated it. I didn't keep up with our "no crying" promise. He had an old pair of shoes that he wore all the time. They were sitting there empty in the closet in front of me. I thought about how big those shoes were, and how impossible it felt to fill them. I just sat there and talked to him. If someone were watching from the outside they would have probably thought I was crazy. I looked over and noticed a pile of old sermon notes he had just laying around and I grabbed the one on top. I can't make this up… In his own hand writing, it has Scripture written on top. James 1:2-4 and reads:

"Consider it all joy, my brethren, when you encounter various trials, knowing that the testing of your faith produces endurance. And let endurance have *its* perfect result, so that you may be perfect and complete, lacking in nothing."

He goes on to talk about when the bottom of our life seems to fall out and we feel like we've been pounded into a corner of doubt and unbelief, we need to remember that we have to have a willingness to accept whatever may come our way, knowing that by God's Grace we can win and come out even stronger. Determine to stand our ground while others are running away. Accept that God is molding you even in the midst of this mess. At the bottom, he simply writes "Don't Quit." It was the single most encouraging thing I've ever read. I don't think it was just randomly sitting there either. God knew what I needed, and who He needed to provide it through. As I sit here and hold that very sheet of paper, I often wonder if my Dad knew that when he wrote these notes, that one day they would help his sons in the time of his death?

" Don't quit "

Dad went through some tough depression years ago. Stress of life and his job as a pastor. He was close to giving up. He called a pastor friend of his and that friend drove three hours to talk to him. My Dad claims it as a turning point in his life. Through all of this, through the accident, through the death of my Dad…it's perfect wisdom and my Dad lived it until the day he went to be with the Lord. That friend said "David, you can't quit. A lot of people depend on you. You know you're a big tree to a lot of people? And when big trees fall, they take a lot of smaller trees with them." I thank God every day that my Dad didn't fall. I thank God every day that I didn't fall. The enemy had me so wrapped up in other things…so distracted. I've learned that it's ok to bend sometimes. You know trees bend. They never break. The big trees never break. I will tell you that whatever you're going through is NEVER too much that God can't handle it. You just have to get yourself to a point in your life where you will let Him handle it. Be who God has called you to be and never look back. Don't Quit. You're a big tree, Ya, know? Don't break. Never. Ever. Break.

God Wins

"Don't quit"

In Memory of my Dad, Dr. David H. Preston, Sr.

BIG TREES NEVER FALL